WORLD'S FAIR COLLECTIBLES

CHICAGO, 1933 AND NEW YORK, 1939

HOWARD M. ROSSEN

Schiffer Publishing Ltd

4880 Lower Valley Rd. Atglen, PA 19310 USA

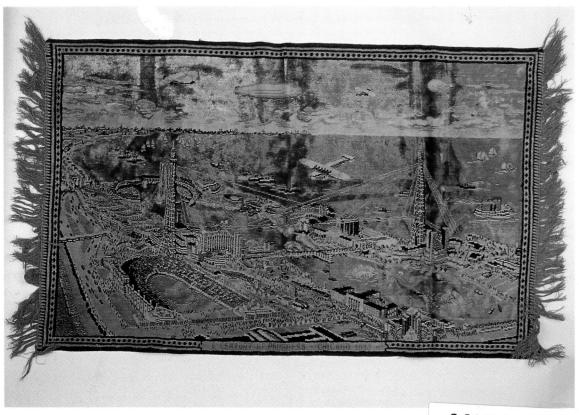

Copyright © 1998 by Howard M. Rossen
Library of Congress Catalog Card Number: 97-80348

DESIGNED BY BONNIE M. HENSLEY

ISBN: 0-7643-0460-7
Printed in China
1 2 3 4

Published by Schiffer Publishing Ltd.
4880 Lower Valley Road
Atglen, PA 19310
Phone: (610) 593-1777; Fax: (610) 593-2002
E-mail: Schifferbk@aol.com
Please write for a free catalog.
This book may be purchased from the publisher.
Please include $3.95 for shipping.

Please try your bookstore first.

We are interested in hearing from authors
with book ideas on related subjects.

DEDICATIONS

Chicago World's Fair

The dedication of the first portion of this book belongs to James (Jim) Moran. A collector extraordinaire, Jim was the proud owner of one of the finest collections of souvenirs from this important event. His longtime collection was housed in the Automobile Museum in Auburn, Indiana for many years before its sale to a private collector three years ago. Visitors, who came to see the cars, were pleasantly surprised when they walked to the second floor and were greeted by an overwhelming display of souvenirs from the Century of Progress. Posters and framed pictures were flanked everywhere by glass showcases filled with hundreds of souvenirs. Items included a full size pinball machine, police and guard uniforms, a life size thermometer from an actual fair exhibit, ladies jewelry, compacts and purses, and much more. Jim often came to the museum to welcome visitors and friends. He was the consummate collector and tour guide. Then and now he continues to share his vast knowledge with everyone interested.

New York World's Fair

The second dedication belongs to my wife, Ellen. She was the encouragement for this book as well as for my first book in 1976 on *Columbian World's Fair Collectibles.* Ellen wrote the text for both fairs presented in this volume and for my prior book. Since I am both a collector and an author, I can appreciate a spouse who understands and tolerates the paranoia associated with compulsive collecting. I proudly dedicate this portion of the book to Ellen Rossen who has provided me with thirty-five years of happiness and aggravation, both ingredients necessary for a successful marriage.

Special thanks also goes to Mark and Diane Bender and Martin Shape for their assistance and encouragement in helping to compile this book. Final thanks to Bill Crowl, known to all collectors of World's Fair materials, for thirty years of friendship and for providing many of the souvenirs in my personal collection. His endless search for this memorabilia has fueled the compulsive nature of this hobby for many of us.

4

CONTENTS

INTRODUCTION

The purpose of this book is to provide a visit to the two most important World's Fairs of the twentieth century. I hope to accomplish this effort by picturing for the readers a wide array of souvenirs available for purchase by visitors at each fair. The range of items for sale is beyond comprehension. From simple ash trays, to ornate woven tapestries, to children's toys, to spectacular posters, the visitor could take home a remembrance of an event that would take its place in history. In many ways it is ironic that both the Chicago and New York World's Fairs would take place during the Great Depression. While both fairs represented a look at the past and present, at the same time they provided hope for the future. One could simply forget his or her worries by visiting the World's Fair and enjoying the myriad of events and amusements. In a sense it was an escape from the hard times of the era. Relive part of the exciting past by visiting the souvenirs presented in the following pages.

Part I
A CENTURY OF PROGRESS
THE CHICAGO WORLD'S FAIR: 1933-34

Opening day poster, 1933, Neely Printing Co. $1,500.

The idea of a giant celebration by Chicago on the occasion of its centennial was supported by Mayor William E. Dever, who, on August 17, 1923 with the support of City Council, appointed a committee of citizens to lay the foundations for the celebration. A group of leaders planning the second World's Fair wanted to repeat the triumph of 1893 and highlight the progress made in Chicago during the century.

On the fifth day of January, 1928, A Century of Progress was organized as an Illinois not-for-profit corporation, having as its charter purpose the holding of a World's Fair in Chicago in the year 1933. The original name of the corporation, "Chicago Second World's Fair Centennial Celebration," was changed on July 9, 1929 to "A Century of Progress."

A Century of Progress was completed without one cent of taxation being imposed upon the citizens. No federal government, state, county, or city subsidy was asked for or received. Early needs were met from the fees of the founding and sustaining members of the corporation: $1,000.00 each for the former and $50.00 each for the latter.

As an expression of their faith in the enterprise, the citizens of Chicago formed the World's Fair Legion. More than a hundred thousand paid the $5.00 membership fee; the total was set aside with a trustee for return to members if the fair never opened or to purchase admission tickets when it did open.

The basis of financing was an issue of gold notes of ten million dollars. These notes were secured by the deposit of forty per cent of the gate receipts in the hands of the trustees and were guaranteed by the endorsement of prominent citizens of Chicago.

The object of the Century of Progress Exposition was to tell in a dramatic way the story of the discoveries and inventions of the past century, their application, and the transformation they effected.

The admission price to enter the fairgrounds was fifty cents for adults and twenty-five cents for children between the ages of three and twelve years. Non-transferable season tickets, providing 150 admissions, could be purchased for $15.00.

Souvenir menus from Olde Heidelberg Inn. $40.

Skyride poster, 1933. $80

Prices for hotel services at first-class hotels near the fair ranged from $1.50 to $5.00 per person a day. The average price for first-class accommodations in the leading hotels was $3.00 a day. In most hotels, meals were fifty cents to $1.00. Many places on the grounds also sold meals and sandwiches, and drinks could be bought on the grounds for between ten and fifteen cents.

If visitors chose to stay in a rooming house or in a private home, the cost was as little as a $1.00 a day or less for long stays.

The great thrill feature of A Century of Progress was the spectacular Skyride. It was a monster Ferris Wheel and everybody was anxious to ride it. Two towers 1,850 feet apart supported the Skyride. Each tower was embedded in cement and rose 628 feet into the sky. There were observation floors on top of the towers and looking down at night you saw a magic city that seemed to float in a vast pool of light.

The rocket cars used for the Skyride were suspended from a cableway which had a breaking strength of 220,000 pounds per square inch of cross section. The rocket cars could handle 5,000 visitors per hour.

House of Tomorrow

One of the interesting parts of the Home Planning Hall exhibit was the circular glass house called the "House of Tomorrow." This house was built around a central mast which contained all utilities. The exterior walls were made of clear glass and had no windows. Drapes, roller and Ve-

8

netian blinds provided privacy. All modern equipment was used and the furniture was especially designed. On the ground floor there was an airplane hanger in addition to the garage. The roof above formed an extensive deck terrace. Ventilation was filtered, washed, heated or cooled air that recirculated every ten minutes.

The house was declared to be a "laboratory" house built for the purpose of determining the attitude of World's Fair visitors to the idea of an utterly different home.

The Midway

The Midway offered an exciting array of choices to explore. You could play games, watch magic tricks, watch youths dive in tanks to wrestle with alligators, or ride the roller coaster. There were beauties of the Orient who danced, and there were wrestlers, fencers, sword fighters, and Egyptian dancers and jugglers. "Living wonders" included the Siamese Twins and giant people. A visit to the Midget Village gave you the opportunity to see how sixty Lilliputians lived. On the Dance Ship were two double-decker dance floors and two orchestras accommodating two thousand or more dancers.

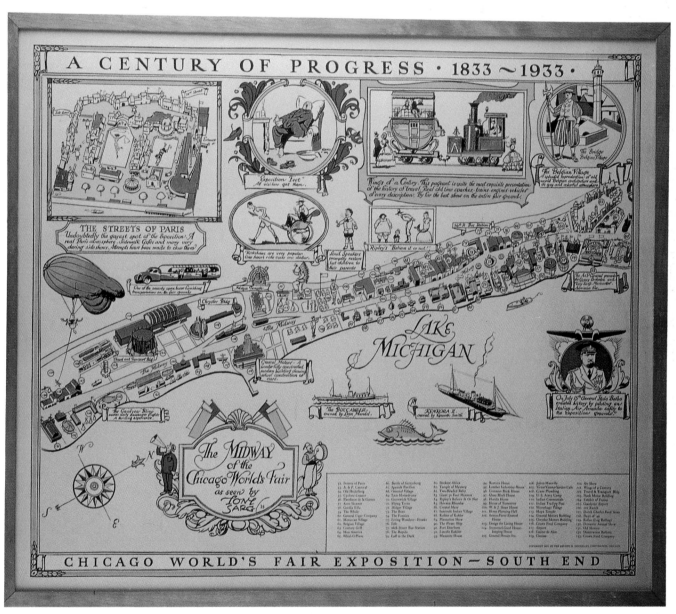

Tony Sarg Midway Map of the 1933 fair. $500.

9

The Streets of Paris and Sally Rand

Left to right: Sally Rand fan dancer statue, 1934, with ostrich feathers, $250; original autographed photo of Rand in costume, $750; Pendulette Clocks of Fort Dearborn, $500, and Sally Rand, $1,000; photo of Rand on the fairgrounds, $250.

A popular attraction was the Streets of Paris. On narrow, stone paved streets were found sidewalk cafes, quaint shops, vendors, strolling artists, and musicians. Amusements included a beauty revue, clowns, a chamber of horrors, and peep shows.

The most famous attraction was the risqué fan dance of Sally Rand. Sally Rand was an unemployed movie actress who tried to get a job at the Chicago World's Fair as Lady Godiva. Although she rode a white horse on the midway minus a costume, she did not convince the fair operators to hire her for that job. Instead, she was hired as a fan dancer with two ostrich feathers comprising her only costume. Sally claimed that wearing any other costume interfered with the movement of her fans. She was an extremely popular fair attraction—seventy-three thousand people watched her act in the first month. Her salary increased from $175 per week to $3,000 per week based on her enormous popularity and the crowds she drew throughout the fair.

Sally Rand's stage show caused a revolution among the religious right and City Hall. Suit was filed to ban the show, but a judge ruled that First Amendment freedoms protected her right to perform. The show continued with standing room only crowds for almost all performances.

Hollywood

In World's Fair Hollywood, motion picture productions were filmed daily and could be watched through a glass before a sixty-foot stage. Outdoor sets surrounding the buildings were available for amateur movie photographers to shoot their own scenes. Some of the subjects filmed were the various motion picture celebrities who visited the fair. "Spectaculum," a three-dimensional picture that gave depth to the characters, was one of the new motion picture special effects shown at the fair.

Belgian Village

To enter the sixteenth century Belgian Village, visitors pulled a latchstring and found themselves in a reproduced Belgian town. Medieval homes, cafes, a fish market, a town hall, and an old church, combined with craftsmen and folk dancers, made visitors feel as if they were actually tourists in long-ago Belgium.

Souvenir motion pictures of attendees to 1933 fair. $200.

Reverse painting on glass tray depicting Belgian Village, 1933. $150.

Old Fort Dearborn

From left: two 1933 Fort Dearborn plaster statues, $50; Fort Dearborn metal statue on base, $75; and copper-plated statue of fort, 1933, $75.

The Fort was completed in every detail to faithfully reproduce the first Fort Dearborn in 1803. A seventy-foot flagpole stood in the center of a quadrangular parade ground. Fifteen stars stood for each of the states in 1812. There was a blockhouse on both corners and narrow slits along the wall where soldiers' trained their guns. The Fort contained officers' quarters, the supply building, and the powder magazine. On a table were sample rations for a day given to soldiers of the time: a pound of flour, a pound of meat, vinegar, a half gill of whisky, salt, and a piece of soap. In the fort store, provisions of the time were reproduced and included jerked beef, skins, knives, calico cloth, and corn meal.

Events for Children at the Fair

For the children attending the fair, five acres were set aside for their own Enchanted Island.

A huge push-wagon stood fifteen feet high with a big boy on its top who moved; underneath was a shop where wagons were made. There was a house of marbles and a children's restaurant. Also on the grounds were a fairy castle, a mechanical zoo, a miniature railroad, a marionette show, and a theater that staged plays. Among the plays staged by the Junior League of Chicago were *Peter Pan*, *Cinderella*, *The Birthday of the Infants*, and *The Ordeal of Sir Garwayne*.

1933 Games. From top left: Master Marbles with leather pouch in original box, $750; picture card accordion, Tumble, Tumble, $100; Game of Nations by Kimbler Novelty Co., $100; wooden Progress Puzzle in original box, $75.

World's Fair Medal

Official 1933 commemorative medals. Large size in original box, $300; medium size in original box, $200; small size in original box, $100; souvenir medal of participating nations on original card with ribbon, $150.

An official World's Fair Medal was designed by Emil Robert Zetter, the head of the industrial arts section of the Art Institute of Chicago. The medal was done in bronze and depicts a strong, swift figure, symbol of energy and action, which represents the intellectual arch between man's resources and man's work. The dates 1833 and 1933 are inscribed on the piece and the figure stands with a foot on each date. The reverse side carries a plan of the World's Fair grounds. The medal came in three sizes: 2 3/4 inches wide, 2 1/4 inches wide, and 1 1/2 inches wide. The first medal struck was for presentation to President Franklin D. Roosevelt.

Conclusion

A Century of Progress was conceived and created to meet all tastes. There were science-oriented activities for those interested in the serious and carnival-type activities for those just looking for fun. There were opportunities for quiet contemplation as well as opportunities for activity, sports, and recreation. Industry was depicted in the story of progress—both of power and art—and music was expressed throughout the fair.

Everyone's needs could find fulfillment at the fair: children, students, young adults, and senior citizens alike.

"Chicago asked the world to join her in celebrating a century of the growth of science, and the dependence of industry on scientific research."

The souvenir items that follow will give the reader and collector a taste of the greatness and variety of this splendid event.

Opening day poster for 1933 by Goes Litho Co. $2,500.

Color variation on opening day 1933 poster. $2,500.

Art Deco scene
poster, 1934, by
Sandor. $1,500.

Wings of a Century, 1933, Neely Printing Co. $1,500.

Go Chicago
poster by Cuneo
Press, Inc., 1933.
$500.

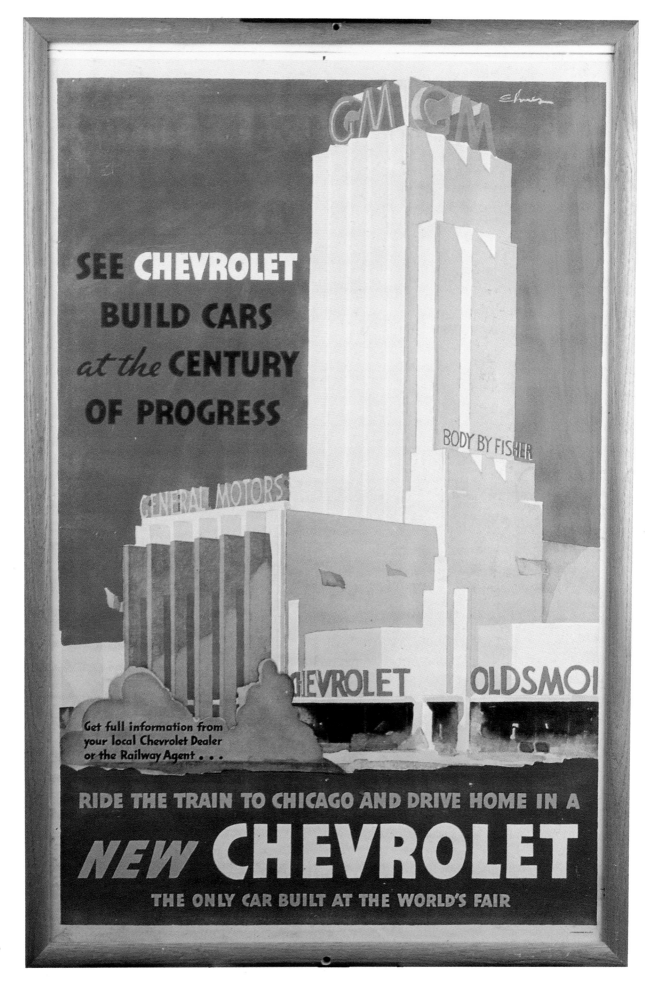

Chevrolet
advertisement,
1933. $1,500.

Opening day from
Canadian Pacific
Railway, 1933
reproduction by
Poster Plus, Inc.
$300.

Ford Exposition poster, 1934. $1,000.

Ticket collage with special passes and tickets to events at 1933-34 fair. $1,000.

Centennial Celebration poster, 1933. $700.

Official set of tickets, 1933. $100.

Tony Sarg map showing north end of Chicago fair, 1933. $500.

Official invitation to the opening ceremonies, 1933. $150.

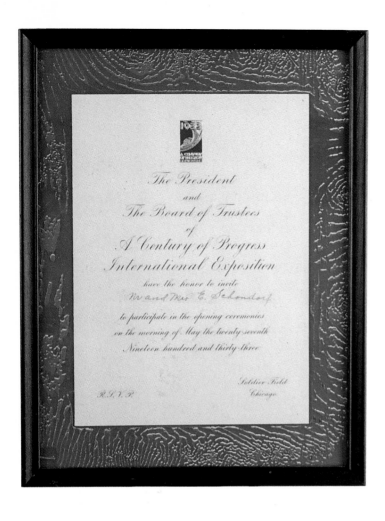

Invitations and badges from 1933: invitations, $50 each; hostess badge, $50; Florida Exhibit business card, $50; visitor's button, $75.

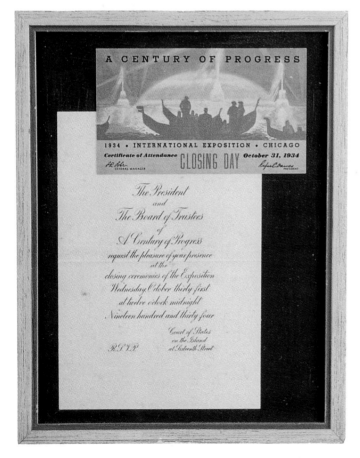

Invitation to the closing ceremonies, 1934. $200.

Above: Stratosphere Ascension exhibit sponsored by Pickard-Compton at 1933 fair. $300.
Below: World's Fair vacation label, 1933. $100.

Attendance certificate to 1933 fair. $150.

Opposite page:
Top: Mediterranean Village visitor's certificate at 1934 fair. $150.
Bottom: Rickshaw attendants with official badge, 1933. $200.

Award certificate presented to exhibitor at 1933 fair. $250.

THE OASIS
MEDITERRANEAN VILLAGE
A CENTURY OF PROGRESS

خَدِيْقَةُ الصَّحْرَاء

نحن حكام حديقة الصحرآ في معرض شيكاغو الواقعة على شواطئ بحيرة
شيغن بالسلطة الملكية الممنوحة لنا كحكام هذه البقعة نعين ونعلن أن
.... من .... اتخذ جنسية الحديقة واصبح
من الصحرآ في يوم ...... من شهر ...... سنة ١٩٣٤

WE, grand rulers of THE OASIS, Mediterranean village at A Century of Progress, on the shores
of Lake Michigan, by the imperial powers conferred upon us as rulers of this domain, do hereby
appoint and proclaim *Alice Early*, of *Sheridan Wyoming* a Citizen
of THE OASIS and a *Dervish*, of the Desert.

Done this *6th* day of *October* the year 1934.

BY TOUFIC BEY

Souvenir guidebooks, 1933-34. $35 each.

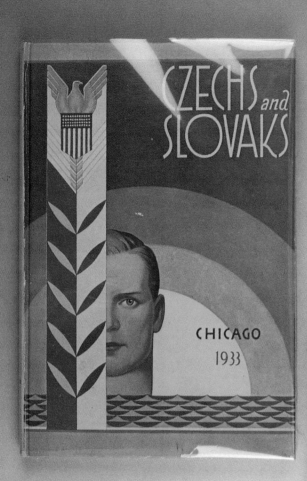

Czechs and Slovaks book, $150; Guide book to Chicago, $40.

Top: Six weekly programs from 1933, $50 each. Bottom: Official World's Fair Weekly subscription form, $25.

Assorted tickets, admission badges, and permits for 1933-34 fair. $25-200.

Opposite page: Assorted items from Midget Village. Clockwise from top left: Official picture frame, $100, with Midget Village catalogue (in frame), $100; celluloid photo mirror featuring four midget musicians called The Little Band, $100; miniature photo of miniature village, $20; modern Lilliputia souvenir edition, $75; Midget Village News from June, 1933, $50; Midget Village felt cap, $100.

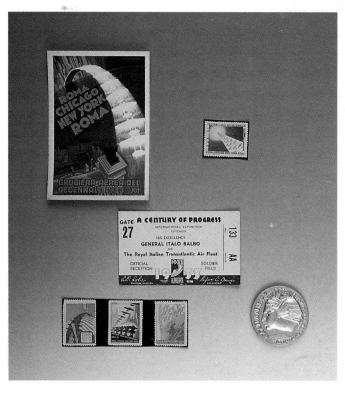

General Balbo Royal Italian Transatlantic Air Fleet souvenirs, 1933: postcard, $25; set of four stamps, $25; admission card to official reception, $100; commemorative medal, $300.

HUGH W. PERKINS   SGT- GUIDE CORPS

THE 1933 YELLOW BATON, 1934 CHROME
BATON, GLOVES AND CORPORAL STRIPES ARE
GIFTS FROM HIM.   1933   — PHOTOS - 1983

THIS UNIFORM MADE FOR
T. GRIFFN
PASS GATE ATTENDANT
AT THE
CENTURY OF PROGRESS.

Gate attendant
uniform complete
with badges, hat,
and key to the
1933 fair. $1,000.

Brinks uniform from 1933
fair. $750.

German-American Bund Friendship badges distributed at the German Pavilion, 1933. Smaller badges, $75; middle badge, $250.

Left to right: Keystone Stereoscope with photographs and original box, 1933, $175; Film Funnies with camera in original box, $200; Picture Film Viewer with original box, $150; Tru-Vue viewer with film, in original mailer box, $150.

Left to right: box camera with fair decal, 1933, $100; Brownie box camera with metal plaque showing fair logo, $150; same with different logo, $150; miniature box camera made in Japan, $100.

36

The dance begins - proud and arched body rising from silvered folds of gossamer -

Poised for an instant - startled by the vision of her own beauty.

Sally Rand Tru-Vue photo poster, 1933. Full poster plus close-ups of individual poses. $2,000.

Light, feathery, airy - soft - caressing - gentle - proud.

Wheeling, turning, floating among the moonbeams on the water -

Bewitched by her own beauty, embracing it, reveling in it -

Away again - gliding, turning, skimming in the silvery light.

Wings fluttering wildly, heart racing madly - pulses pounding.

Travel and Transportation Building metal lamp. $250.

Left to right: Federal Building lamp with matching shade, 1933, $250; two-piece glass lamp with decals, 1934, $175; Travel and Transportation Building metal lighting fixture, 1933-34, $250; Copper-plated !amp depicting Travel and Transportation Building, 1933, $250.

Playing cards: Belgian Village deck, $100; official logo deck, 1934, $75; Hall of Science deck, $50; Hall of Science deck, $50; Skyride deck, $75; official logo, $75; Belgian Village, $50; Avenue of Flags, $75; Avenue of Flags in red, green, and yellow, $75; Belgian Village, $100.

Playing cards, 1933: Double deck from the Walgreen Building, $100; Belgian Village, $50; Hall of Science, $50; brass double deck card holder, $100; double deck bridge set in leather pouch, $150; Skyride deck, $75; Travel and Transportation Building, $75; fair logo, $75; same; 1934 deck with official logo, $75; purple logo deck, 1934, $75.

39

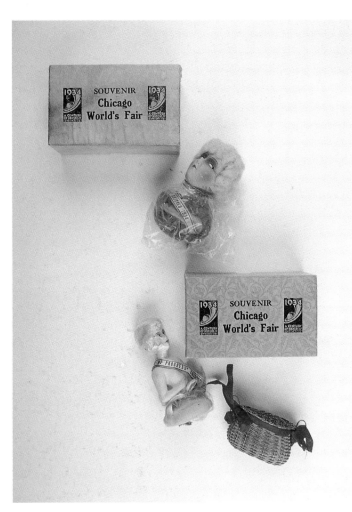

Doll heads in original boxes. $150 each.

Top to bottom: Clothes brush with wooden child plaque, $100; figural dog head brush, $150; ladies figural dust brush in original box, 1933, $150.

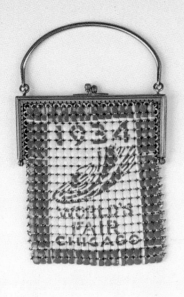

Ladies miniature purses. Left to right: green and white beaded purse, $300; blue mesh metal handbag showing Fort Dearborn, by Whiting & Davis Co. $500; black and white beaded purse, $300.

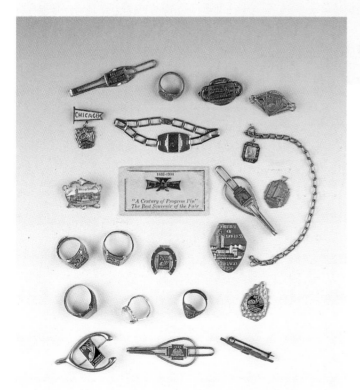

Fair jewelry, 1933, including rings, tie bars, and pins. $25-50.

Opposite page:
Top: Leather souvenirs: brown leather wallet showing Travel and Transportation Building, $50; leather pencil case, $50; leather scrapbook showing Skyride, $75; two black leather wallets showing Hall of Science, $75 each.

Bottom: Additional leather souvenirs: Center: leather book cover, $75. Clockwise, from top left: Skyride scrapbook, $75; ladies purse showing Fort Dearborn, $75; leather mirror and comb holder, $75; leather change purse showing Fort Dearborn, $50; whisk broom in leather case, $50; leather key case, $50; leather handkerchief box showing Belgian Village, $75.

Century of Progress ladies' compacts by manufacturers including Zell, Elgin-American, Girey, and others, 1933-34. $50-$300.

43

24 karat gold-plated table setting pieces: candy dishes, 1933-34, $140; salt and pepper serving set, 1933, $150; covered sugar, 1933, $150; matching creamer, 1933, $150; creamer, 1933, $150; 1934 candy dish with handle, depicting Temple of Jehol, $150; dinner plate depicting Temple of Jehol, 1933, manufactured by Hutschenreuther and made in Bavaria, $250.

Left to right: Federal Building and Hall of States, 1933, made by Ridgways, England, $150; large Ford Pavilion plate by Shenango China Co., 1933, $150; small Ford Pavilion plate by Shenango China Co., 1933, $100; US and Swedish flag plate, made in Sweden, 1933, $150; Anton Cermak Plate, 1933, by Edwin Knowles China Co., $300.

Round scalloped plates, 1933, depicting Travel Building, Federal Building, and Carillon Tower, by Pickard. $75 each.

Square scalloped plates, 1933-34, depicting Carillon Tower, Hall of Science, and Belgian Village, by Pickard. $75 each.

Above: Scalloped plates, depicting Belgian Village and Temple of Jehol, by The Salem China Co., 1934. $75 each.
Below: Scalloped plates depicting Travel and Transportation Building and US Government Building, by The Salem China Co., 1934. $75 each.

Above: Pitchers depicting Hall of Science and Travel Building in Chicago, by Pickard, 1934, $200 each; scalloped plate showing Federal Building, 1933, by Pickard, $75.
Below: Pottery. Left to right: pottery vase, 1934, $175; pottery vase with relief depiction of Hall of Science, 1933, $125; two-handled vase, 1934, $150.

Left to right: lusterware cup depicting Czechoslovakian Pavilion, 1933, $125; pottery stein by Canonsburg Pottery Co., 1933, $150; brown pottery stein depicting Chicago, 1933, $75; Stewart & Ashby Coffee cup, made by Shenango China Co., 1933, $75.

Above: Left to right: 1933 Pottery beer stein with fair logo, $175; pottery beer stein, made in Germany, 1933, $175; large pottery beer stein with relief work and hand-painted color, made in Japan, 1933, $150.
Below: Left to right: black glass vase incised "World's Fair, 1934," $175; blue glass tulip vase, 1933, $100; green glass tulip vase, 1933, $100; World's Fair candle holder with blue glass vase, $150; blue glass scalloped tulip vase, 1933, $100; black glass tulip vase, 1933, $100; clear glass tumbler depicting Mayor Cermak and FDR, 1933, $150.

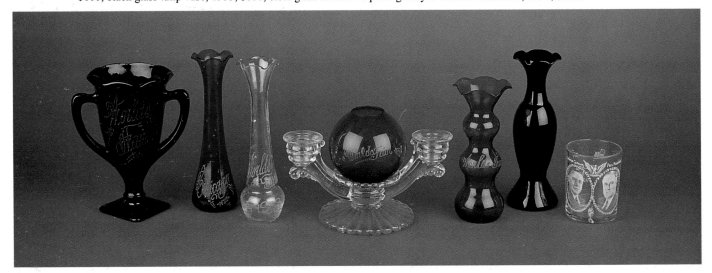

1933 World's Fair pottery steins with relief figures and figural handles: cream and brown, brown, and green. $200 each.

Above: Left to right: 1933 Electrical Building blue-on-white pottery mug by Pickard, $125; large frosted glass mug with 1933 fair logo, $150; 1933 Hall of Science green-on-white pottery mug by Pickard, $125.
Below: Glass mug depicting Hall of Science, shown with four beer glasses depicting Carillon Tower, Antarctic Ship, Administration Building, and Fort Dearborn. $75 each.

Facsimile page of psalter printed on Gutenberg Press for exhibit at 1933 fair. $250.

Facsimile page of Gutenberg Bible printed on Gutenberg Press for exhibit at 1933 fair. $250.

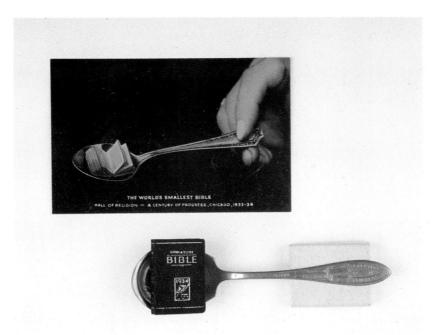

"World's Smallest Bible," 1934, $150; black and white picture postcard of same, $35; and gold-plated spoon with fair logo and embossed handle, $50.

Opposite page:
Top: Left to right: salt and pepper shakers in plastic from the Durkee exhibit, $50; green plastic shakers showing Hall of Science building, $40; glass shakers, 1933, $50; yellow plastic and glass shakers, 1934, $50; orange and black plastic shakers from the Durkee exhibit, $50.
Center: Left to right: Frosty beer mug salt and pepper shakers, 1933, $50; Ball Jar shakers in original box, 1933, $75; Ford Exhibit shakers in original mailing box, $150; Hall of Science metal shakers, 1933, $50; Hall of Science pitcher-shaped metal shakers, 1933-34, $50; wooden barrel shakers, 1934, $50; metal salt shaker, 1934, $35.

From top: Burton Holmes souvenir motion picture film in original box, $150; Burton Holmes souvenir 16mm film in metal canister, $500; souvenir motion picture film, 1934, by Kaufmann and Fabry, $150.

Sears World's Fair model radio in wooden case, 1933, silvertone. $800.

Stewart-Warner Companion Radio, 1933. $900.

Badges. Top row, from left: Founder Member badge, 1933, $100; Gate Supervisor badge, $200. Bottom row, from left: Guide badge, $150; Chair Guide badge, $150.

1933 scrapbooks with
silver inlay of World's
Fair buildings. $100 each.

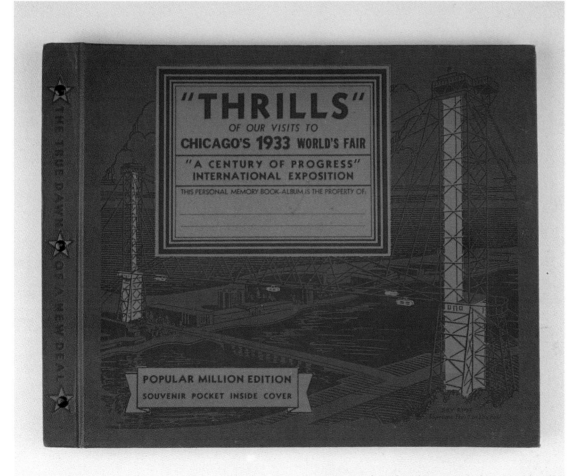

Scrapbook, "Thrills of
Our Visit." Mint
condition. $175.

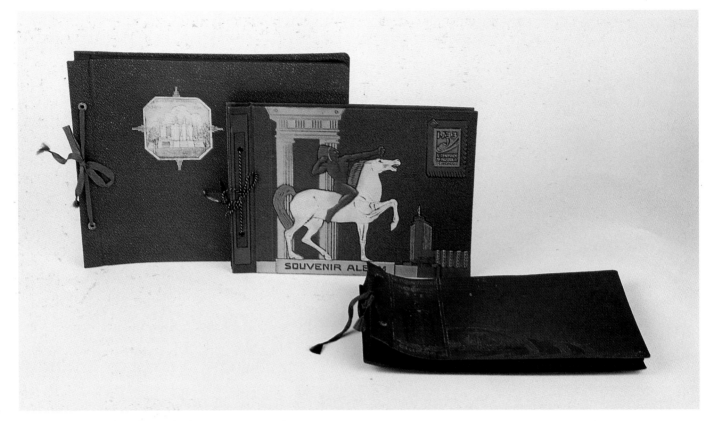

Left to right: large scrapbook with gold decal inlay, 1934, $125; scrapbook featuring Indian on horseback and fair logo, $100; scrapbook depicting Federal Building and Fort Dearborn, 1933, $75.

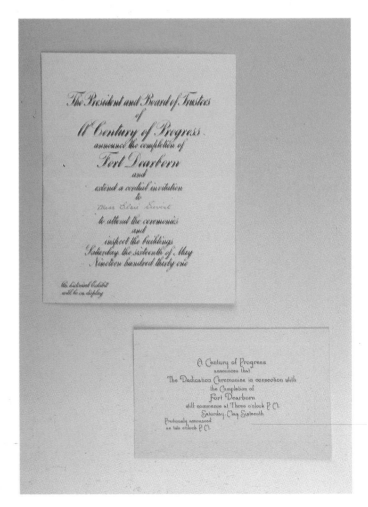

Above: Chicago World's Fair paper parasol in original box from Marshall Field & Co. $175.
Right: Engraved invitation and announcement card for Fort Dearborn opening ceremonies. $60 each.

54

Left to right: red book bank depicting World's Fair logo, 1933, $150; black book bank depicting main entrance to Administration Building, 1933, $150; Travel and Transportation Building metal bank, 1933, $250; American Can Co. giveaway bank in final form and preform, 1934, $100; World's Fair Globe Bank, 1933, $150; wooden barrel bank, 1933, $50; American Can Co. giveaway bank, $50; miniature green luggage bank, 1933, $150.

Porcelain donkey bank made in Japan. $75.

1933 Timepieces: Color dial pocket watch with Federal Building, $500; Waltham pocket watch with logo dial, $500; Ingersoll pocket watch with embossed back, $500; Ingersoll pocket watch with different dial and embossed back, $500; Fort Dearborn dial pocket watch with embossed back in original box, $800; Westclox pocket watch, 1934, with original box, $1,000.

Front: metal sundial by Lannon Quarries Co., 1933, $300. Back, left to right: Middlebury electric clock depicting Hall of Science, 1933, $400; three 1934 Hall of Science mechanical clocks, black, green, and beige, $350; engraved metal desk clock made in Czechoslovakia, 1934, $300.

Paperweight souvenirs: Front row, from left: large glass paperweight featuring Mickey Mouse, 1933, $300; metal paperweight in shape of fair logo with eagle, $100. Back row, from left: silver globe paperweight, 1934, $100; handcut crystal paperweight from the Czechoslovakian Pavilion, $175; paperweight ship, 1933, $75.

Giant Studebaker metal car from 1934 Century of Progress in original box, $700; Chrysler Airflow cars from 1933 in blue and red, $400 each.

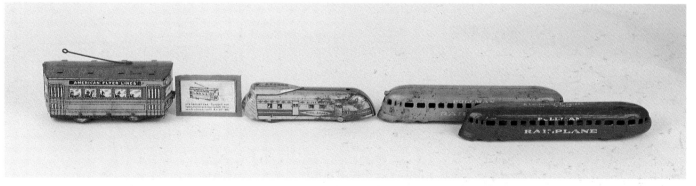

American Flyer trolley car, 1933, $500; Silver Streak mail coach tin car, 1933, $300; two cast iron Pullman Railplane passenger cars in olive and red, $800 each.

57

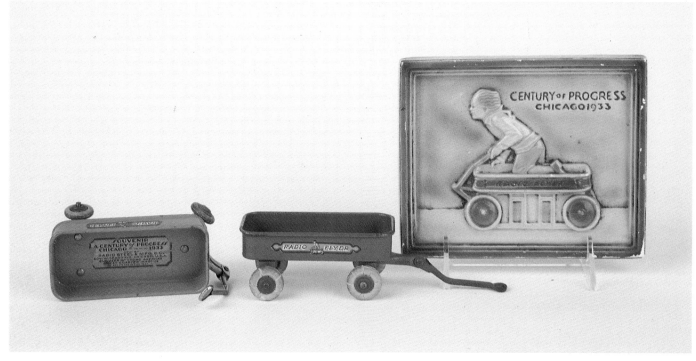

Toy Radio Flyer wagons in orange and green, $200 each; Radio Flyer ceramic plaque from 1933 fair, $500.

Arcade Greyhound cast iron buses: smallest is 5", 1934, $300; 7", 1934, $300; 10", 1933, $400; 11", 1933, $600; and 13", 1933, $1,500. Shown with Greyhound bus driver's hat badge with fair logo, $500; World's Fair Greyhound bus line tickets, $25 each; Greyhound bus line schedules, 1933-34, $35 each.

Toy guns from 1933: toy pistol that shoots rubberbands, $300; toy gun that shoots paper, with original box, $300; Lone Star Ranger cap gun with leather holster, caps, and silver bullets, $400.

Five-piece toy train set in original box, Overland Flyer, 1933. $1,200.

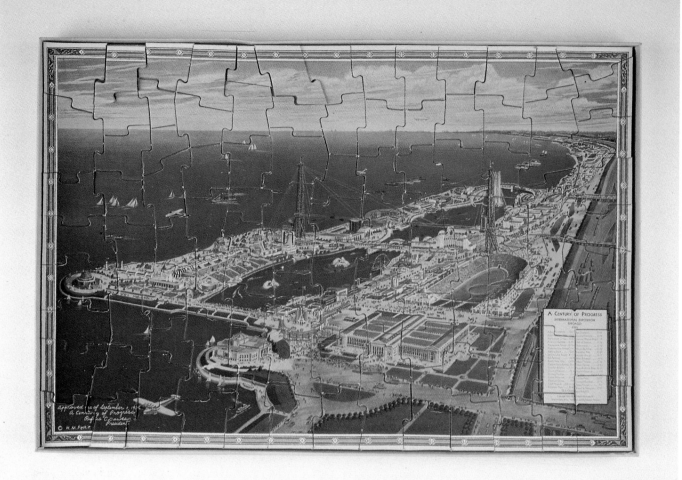

World's Fair
Picture Puzzle
panorama, 1933.
$150.

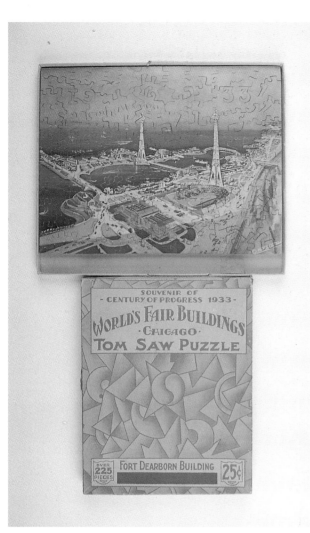

Top: wooden jigsaw puzzle showing panorama of the fair, $150.
Bottom: puzzle of Fort Dearborn Building, 1933, $125.

Fort Dearborn Lincoln Log construction set in original box, 1933, $250.

Reverse painting on glass tray depicting Fort Dearborn, 1933. $150.

Reverse painting on glass tray depicting Federal Building, 1933. $150.

Above: Laminated wooden tray with fair logo and scene of Travel and Transportation Building, 1934. $150.

Below: Tin tray with six matching coasters showing 1933 fair buildings. $300.

Above: Photo reels, 1933. $50 each.

Right: From top: candy box with pictorial view of fair, 1933, $50; packing box with view of fair buildings and the Boston Store, $50; fair photo, 1934, with mother, daughter, and dog, $50.

Below: Mrs. Snyders two-pound chocolate box, $50; Fair Faces hand decorated candies, intact in original box, $100; Wonder Bread wrapper, baked at the fair, $150; World's Fair Pretzel, in original box, from the Black Forest Village, $100.

64

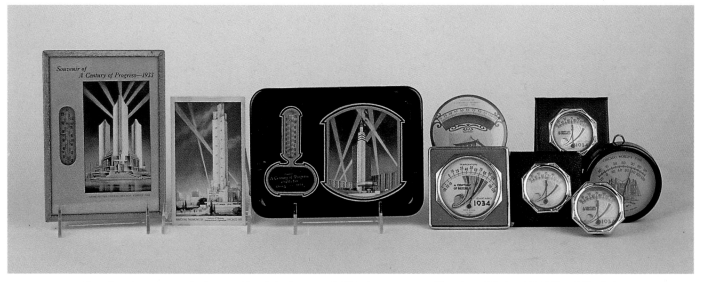

Havoline thermometer in frame with original postcard, $50; thermometer with scene of Federal Building, $50; desk thermometer with scene of Lama Temple, $50; desk thermometer, 1934, $75; desk thermometer in leather case, 1933, $50; desk thermometer in leather case, 1934, $50; hanging thermometer with Travel and Transportation Building, $50; and small desk thermometer in metal case, 1934, $50

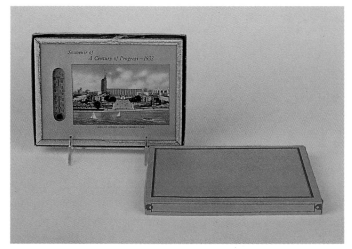

Framed glass thermometer showing Hall of Science, 1933, in original box. $75.

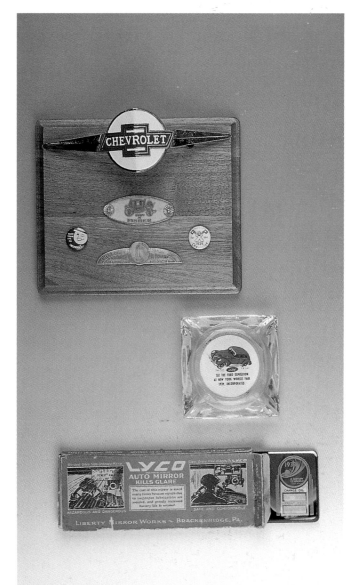

From top: original automotive plaques for General Motors mounted on hardwood board, $300; ashtray from Ford Exhibit, $50; auto mirror by Lyco in original box, $100.

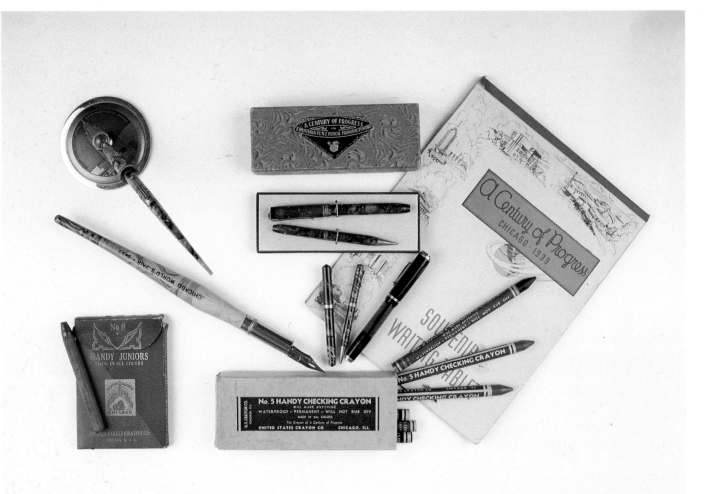

Above: Writing items: desk pen on circular brass base showing Hall of Science, $250; pen and pencil set in original box by Marine Corp., $200; miniature pen and pencil set, $150; Sager fountain pen, $150; oversize wooden dip pen, $100; Handy Juniors crayons by U.S. Crayon Co., $100; Handy Checking crayons by U.S. Crayon Co., $100; souvenir writing tablet, $75.

Below: Burwood desk pen holder with mirror, 1933, $75; metal desk calendar, 1933, $100; another metal desk calendar, 1933, $75.

From left: two ashtrays showing Walgreen's Drugstore, in original boxes, $75 each; Armour Building ashtray in original box, $50.

From left: pot metal crumb tray set in original box, $50; enameled ashtray, $40; ashtray with sand from Lake Michigan, $75; and tin ashtray with enameled 1933 fair logo, $40.

From left: White Owl Cigar box in original mailer, $50; cigarette holder and ashtray, $100; original pack of Century of Progress cigarettes, $75; pot metal cigarette dispenser made in Japan, $100; silver-plated cigarette lighter, 1934, $100; cigarette lighter with 1933 fair logo, $100; corncob pipe, $75; cigarette case and lighter combination, $150; enameled cigarette case, $150; tabletop lighter in shape of camel, $100.

Brass ashtray from the Italian Village, 1934, $50; four glass matching ashtrays in original box by John Ellis & Bro.,
$150; copper ashtray from Chrysler Pavilion with original box, $40; ashtray with fair logo, $40; marble ashtray with
bust of FDR, $100; tin ashtray from Chrysler Pavilion in original box, $50; pot metal ashtray from Japan, $25;
Firestone rubber tire with glass ashtray, 1934, $50; brass ashtray showing Skyride in original box, $75; enameled
ashtray, 1933, $50.

Jumbo cigar in original box, 1933. $150.

Enameled, plastic, and wooden cigarette cases, $50-250 each;
cigarette lighter, 1934, $100; wooden matchbox holders, $50 each;
two packs of matches, $25 each.

Abraham Lincoln metal statue, 1933. $75.

Lincoln Exhibit souvenirs: ink blotter with plaque affixed to cover, $75; ashtray, $50; bookmark, $50; ashtray with Lincoln's birthplace, $75; clay bust from his birthplace, $100; three souvenir pennies, $50 each; brass ashtray with bust, $75; small glass hatchet made at Lincoln Exhibit, $100.

Bakelite canes from 1933 by Gucci. $300 each.

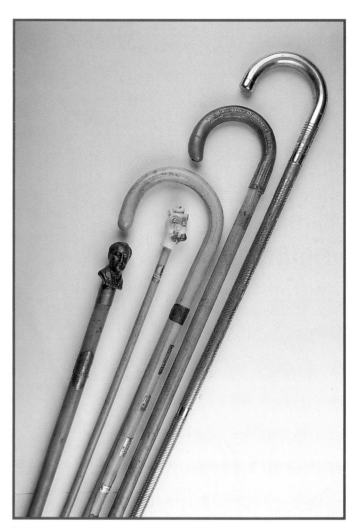

1933 canes: wooden cane with bust of FDR, $150; cane with decal and porcelain head of pig, $100; wooden cane with eight metal insignias affixed, $250; cane with metal engraved handle, $125; aluminum cane with scenes of fair buildings, $200.

1933-34 bracelets: blue enamel from English Village, $50; copper children's, $75; white pot metal children's with fair logo, $75; brass ladies bracelet showing buildings in downtown Chicago, $50; German silver ladies bracelet with scenes of buildings, $75; and stainless steel showing Hall of Science, $50.

Top left: Sheet of commemorative 1-cent stamps, 1933. $50.

Top right: Sheet of commemorative 3-cent stamps, 1933. $50.

Bottom left: Canceled first day covers showing 1933-34 issue of new stamps. Set of 1- and 3-cent covers, $55; Zeppelin first-day cover, $150.

Two 1933 jewelry boxes, one with color scene of 1933 fair, one showing Hall of Science and Transportation Building. $75 each.

Top: complete card of stamped-out souvenir pennies showing 1933 fair logo, $250. Bottom: Colorado one-ounce silver dollar in original holder, 1933, $150.

From left: metal hat for Presidential candidate Al Smith, $75; battery flashlight, tin, $75; small faux wood ink bottle, $50; miniature beer keg advertising piece, $50; same, $50; wooden tumbler, $50; wooden egg sewing kit, $50; silver bullet canister, 1934, $50; paper candy box, $40; brass desk giant paper clip, $50; tin desk plaque showing Fort Dearborn, $50.

Log decanter with three matching cups, 1934. $150.

Celluloid mirrors and tape measures, 1933-34: small mirrors in color and black and white, $50 each; large paperweight mirrors, $100 each; celluloid tape measures, $60.

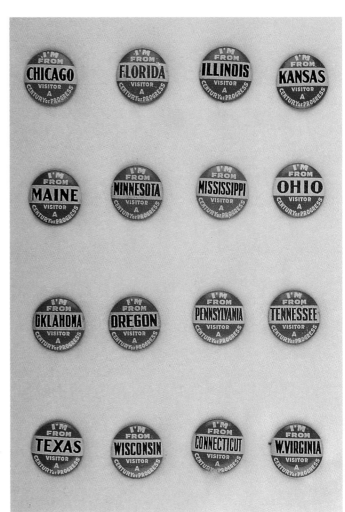

Celluloid pin backs, buttons and belt buckle, 1933-34. $25-100 each.

Metal pin back buttons announcing visitors' home states. $50 each.

Enamel napkin rings depicting World's Fair buildings. $50 each.

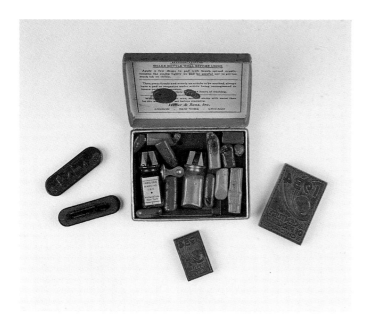

Printing kit, $100; printing stamp in plastic case, $50; small printer's die, $100; large printer's die, $200.

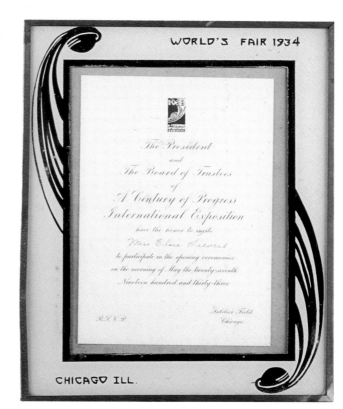

Plaque from Czechoslovakian Pavilion, 1933. $200.

Official picture frame for 1934 fair with engraved invitation to opening ceremonies. $250.

Opposite page:
Top: From left: 1934 Hall of Science bookends, $100 for set; Italian Village Leaning Tower of Pisa, $75; bust of FDR, 1933, $100; statue of Hall of Science, $75; Majestic Radio metal bank, $125; matching bookend, $150.

Center: Copper tray showing Travel Building, 1933, $35; two Burwood plaques showing Federal Building and Hall of Religion, $25 each; three copper-plated coasters showing Electrical Group, Fort Dearborn, and Jehol Temple, 1934, $15 each; round copper tray showing all 1934 fair buildings, $40; copper and wood cigarette box, 1933, $35; copper bookend showing Travel building, 1934, $35.

Bottom: Pot metal souvenirs from Japan including trays, boxes, creamers, sugars, and small vases depicting various fair scenes from 1933. $25 each.

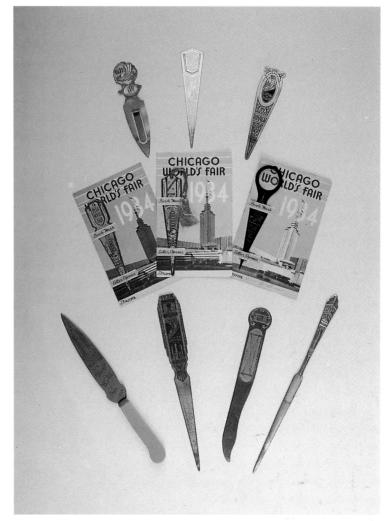

Right: Bookmarks and letter openers from 1933-34. $50-100 each.

Below: Key to the city; assorted keys in metal, 1933. $50-100 each.

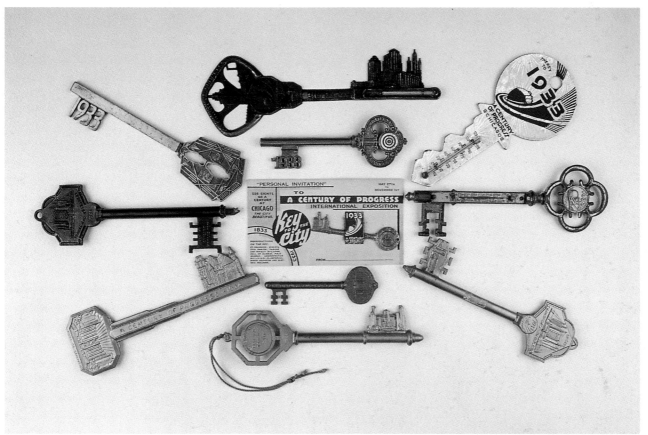

77

Chicago World's Fair Series Diamond Book match covers, set of 10. $100.

Watch fobs: FDR watch fob, $150; official medal, $100; Hungarian Day, $100; Christopher Columbus, $100; American Legion Day, $100; scalloped Century of Progress, $100; logo, $100.

Ladies face powder in original cardboard container, $100; assorted shells, $100; manmade materials from the Ford Exhibit, $100; darning tool in original box, $75; incense from Lama Temple, $100.

License plate ornaments and plaques: Star license plate ornament by Art Forge Inc., $150; large brass plaque showing Fort Dearborn, $250; star license plate ornament by Art Forge, Inc., $150; star plaque, $150; plaque showing Miss Chicago and city scene, made by Majestic Novelty Co., $200; World's Fair Booster license plate ornament in aluminum, $250.

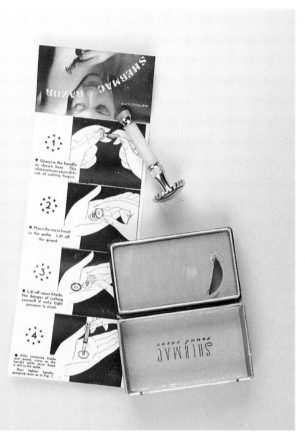

Ladies round razor by Shermac in original box with instructions, 1933. $100.

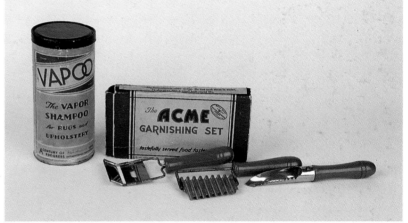

Vapoo Shampoo for carpets in original container, 1934, $75; Acme three-piece garnishing set in original box, $100.

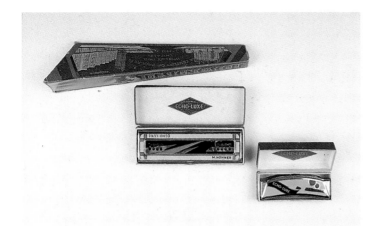

From top: Design-o-Scope kaleidoscope, $200; large harmonica by Hohner in original box, $350; small harmonica by Hohner in original box, $250.

World's Fair fans: Eastern Star folding paper fan, 1933, $100; cardboard folding fan with fair scenes, $100; Chinese fan with family scene, $100; metal folding fan, $150.

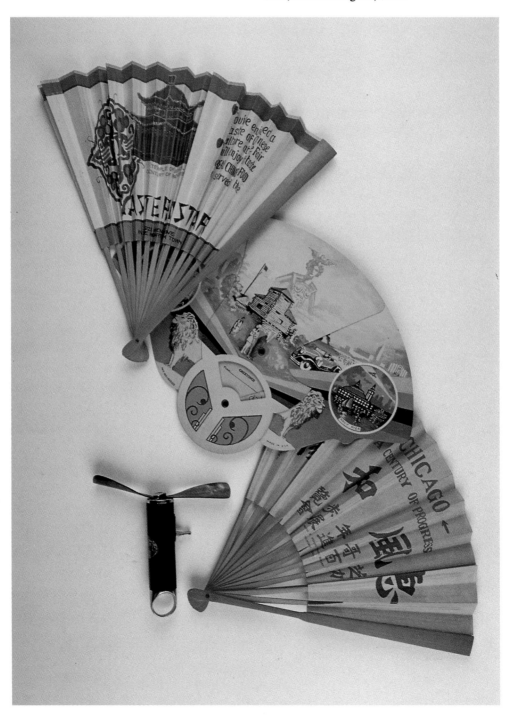

Back row, from left: felt cap with fair logo, $75; green felt cap with 4-H club logo, $75; black felt children's hat, 1934, $75. Front row, from left: ladies souvenir shoes, 1933, $150; children's leather shoes made in Turkey, souvenir of 1933 fair, $100.

Celluloid clothing brush showing Hall of Science in original Marshall Field & Co box, 1933, $100; celluloid clothing brushes from 1933 and 1934, $75 each; large celluloid hanging plaque showing major buildings at the fair, 1933, $150.

Above: Clockwise from left: Figural clothing brush in original box, $150; Dutch Boy doll in original clothing and wooden shoes, $250; wooden plaque from Hungary exhibit, 1933, $100; aluminum folding drinking cup showing Flag of Nations on lid, $75; three gold-plated sugar spoons with fair logo on handles, $50 each; two sterling silver children's spoons, $100 each; Toby stein made in Germany with fair logo, $150; tin globe pencil sharpener, 1933, $100.

Below: From left: wooden horseshoe souvenir, $25; wooden candle with holder, $35; Jack in a Box, $50; one-tenth pint souvenir gin bottle, $50; wooden beer keg, $50; tin top hat made in Japan, $50; hand carved wooden penguin, $25.

1933 Felt pennants: large with Hall of Science, $100; square with Belgian Village, $100; miniature pennant, $25.

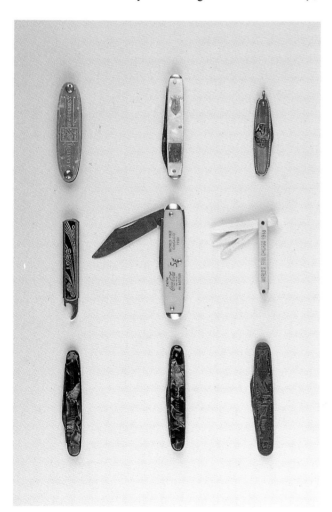

1933 fair pocket knives and bottle opener. $50-150 each.

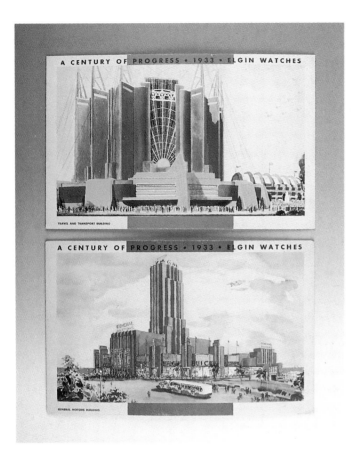

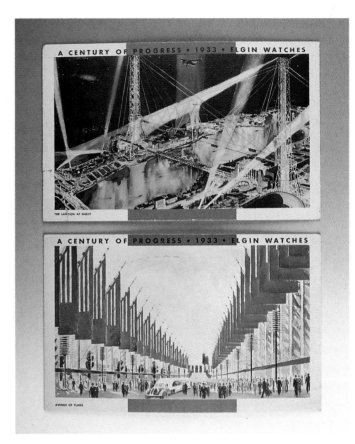

Elgin Watch advertising placards showing General Motors Building and Travel and Transportation Building. $50 each.

Elgin Watch advertising placard showing Avenue of Flags and Lagoon at Night. $50.

Elgin Watch advertising placard showing General Exhibits Building. $50.

Printed handkerchief, 1933. $100.

Silk scarf showing flags of nations at 1933 fair.
$400.

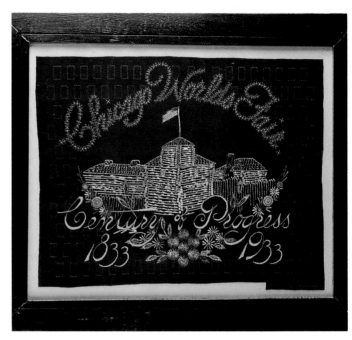

Rayon pillow sham with fair buildings, 1933. $75.

Needlepoint tapestry of Fort Dearborn, 1933, by Mittermaier & Co. $500.

Multi-colored tapestry, 1933. $400.

Tapestry showing panorama view of 1933 fair. $250.

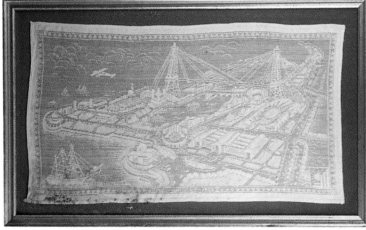

Lace table runner showing scene of 1934 fair. $250.

Rayon bedroom curtains from 1933. $250.

Part II
THE WORLD OF TOMORROW
THE NEW YORK WORLD'S FAIR, 1939-40

World of Tomorrow, 1939, Grinnell Litho Co. $900.

ington was the first President under that Constitution and was inaugurated in New York on April 30th, 1789. The New York World's Fair opened April 30th, 1939, exactly 150 years after George Washington took the oath of office. To honor him, the central avenue of the fair was named Constitution Mall and a sixty-five foot statue of Washington, the great leader in war and peace, was erected there. There was a definite purpose to this fair. It was to foster universal peace and progress by "building the world of tomorrow with the tools of today." The "tools of today" were presented in a myriad of different applications, all hoping to hint at the wonders and contributions to the future welfare of mankind and the unity of all people.

The theme of the fair, "Building the World of Tomorrow," was evident in the architectural line and mass, paint

Attendance certificate in original mailer. $100.

1939 was the year chosen by the organizers of the New York World's Fair because they were interested in linking together three things: the past, the present, and tomorrow. An event of great importance to North America had occurred in New York 150 years before. It was 1789 and the Revolutionary War had resulted in the British colonies becoming independent states. They had united and created a Federal government under a Constitution. George Wash-

and stone, ornament, and speed and labor saving contrivances.

The peace theme of the fair was emphasized through inscriptions on the buildings. Quoted on the Communications Building, for example, were the words, "Modern means of Communication span continents, bridge oceans, annihilate time and space. Servants of freedom of thought and action, they offer to all men the wisdom of the ages to free them from tyrannies and establish co-operation among the peoples of the earth."

A Tour of the Fair

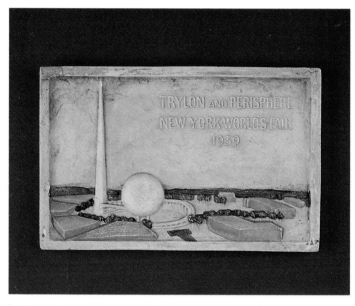

Plaster plaque of T&P, 1939. $200.

The most prominent feature of the New York fair was the gleaming needle-shaped Trylon, seven hundred feet high. Next to it stood a great hollow globe, the Perisphere, two hundred feet in diameter. The Perisphere was an engineering marvel, built for utility as well as for effect. The Trylon and Perisphere (T&P), along with a long curving ramp known as the Helicline, constituted the Theme Center of the 1939 New York World's Fair.

The Perisphere and Trylon were popularized in ornaments and novelties of every description. They were reproduced in jewelry, fabrics, toys, and decorative schemes.

The big ball seemed to float, even though it weighed more than nine million pounds. Located inside the Perisphere was a perfectly integrated garden city of tomorrow which you entered from the side of the Perisphere, fifty feet above the ground, reached by escalators from the Trylon. When visitors entered the magic ball, they found themselves on a slowly revolving platform. Below was the city of tomorrow, one of the largest miniature model cities ever built and the first to portray a full-sized metropolis. Its name was "Democracity."

Things to See at the Fair

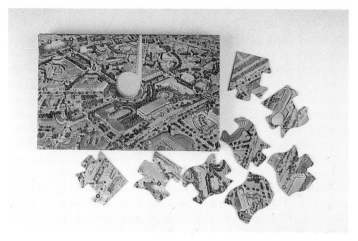

Heavy cardboard puzzle showing panorama of 1939 fair. $150.

There were several unusual things waiting for visitors to see at the fair. You could bail out of a parachute tower from an elevation of 250 feet to a landing below. You could visit a model of the human eye, so large you could actually walk inside it. There was a floor made of cotton and a city populated by little people. Visitors could go to an island populated by penguins or pray in a temple for all religions. A "rocket gun" was shown as a future way to shoot to the moon or Mars. Fireworks were set to music in different patterns. "Steve Brodie" jumped six times a day from a reproduction Brooklyn Bridge. Excitement greeted the visitor at every turn.

Food Concessions

There was no lack of choice for fair-goers looking for meals or snacks. Among the many companies and restaurants represented at the fair were:

Brass Rail, Inc. - restaurant
Casino of Nations - flew the flags of the thirty-two nations participating in the fair
Children's Companys - wholesome type food
Mayflower Doughnut Corporation - lunch counter which serviced from five hundred to eight hundred persons
Toffenette Restaurant - tempting food at popular prices
Turf Trylon - dining facilities for 650 patrons on an outdoor terrace and mezzanine.
Borden Company - milk stands
Roy & Dunlap Frozen Custard - custard, hotdogs, and hamburgers
Refreshment at the Fair - Coca-Cola stands
Richardson Corporation - root beer
State Popcorn Products, Inc. - twenty-five popcorn stands
Sutter Candy Company - salt water taffy
Union News Company - dairy products

Other Concessions Located at the Fair to Accommodate Visitors' Needs and Desires

Assorted pictorial postcards in color, with original mailer, 1939. $150.

Stuart Brooks - Red Cross Brand shoes. Shoes retailed at $6.50 a pair and slippers at $1.95. Handbags and gloves could be purchased from $2.95.

Exposition Souvenir Corporation - fifty stands selling novelties, postcards, view books, view folders.

Faber, Coe & Gregg, Inc. - cigars, cigarettes, nuts, candies, and chewing gum.

Frank Galland - there were fifteen "Penny Crusher" units in various sections of the grounds. Visitors could have their pennies embossed with fair-approved designs at a charge of five cents.

Kaplan & Bloom - canes and umbrellas.

Penny Fortune Scales - there were two hundred penny weighing scales on the fairgrounds.

Photomatic Studios - Two large studio buildings and several studios in buildings at the fair.

Nestle Milk Chocolate Round in original box, $100; Photomatic views of visitors at the fair, $50 each; Bromo-Seltzer miniature picture book, 1939, $50; Gold Key Contest envelope with key and instruction card for auto giveaway at the fair, $50; fair key with thermometer, 1939, $50; glass swizzle sticks, $40 each.

Admissions

Leather booklet of season tickets complete with identification card of New York State Senator, 1939, $150; season ticket/pass with button, $75; metal identification tags, $50 each.

There were no free passes or complimentary tickets for entrance to the fair. Regular admission was seventy-five cents for adults and twenty-five cents for children. On one special day per week children were admitted for ten cents.

If an adult wanted a season ticket , his or her photograph was taken and a non-transferable ticket issued for $15.00. For children, the cost was $5.00.

Facts About the Fair

The New York World's Fair lacked for nothing in the way of offering services and conveniences to those who attended.

There were almost two thousand members of a specially trained and uniformed World's Fair Police.

Over one thousand public telephones and booths were installed in subway and railroad stations, rest rooms, concessions stands, and at the entrances and exits to buildings.

Parents could locate lost children at the headquarters of the Department of Housing and Welfare. Children were cared for by specially trained policemen until parents were located.

Seventeen information booths were located at the fair entrances as well as at strategic points on the grounds.

Amusements

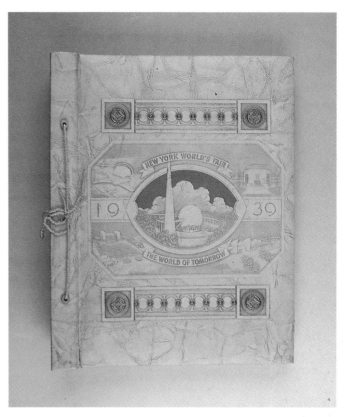

New York World's Fair scrapbook. $100.

Similarly, there was no lack of amusement in the 280 acres set aside for the enjoyment of visitors from all over the world. Every type of amusement was featured—the romantic, the realistic, the unique, the weird, the impressive, and the fantastic.

Among the exciting choices for those visiting the fair were:

Admiral Byrd's Penguin Island - Admission was ten cents to see the miniature island where the penguins dove, slid, and caught fish.

Amazons In No Man's Land - Grecian enclosures were the setting for tall young athletic women who displayed the harmony and beauty of the perfect feminine physique in action.

Bobsled - Visitors hurled at terrific speeds down a banked runway. Turns were taken at stomach-jolting ninety degree angles. Admission was twenty-five cents.

In addition, there were several exciting amusement rides set up for visitors to enjoy at the Fair. The Silver Streak traveled at sixty miles an hour around a circular track. A single unit car held sixty people.

Skee Ball and Chine Ball used the very latest in bowling equipment and attracted devotees of nine pins who were able to try their skill on regulation alleys for only five cents a ball.

The Snapper was another tub ride, with six people to a tub. The cars wove in and out, criss-crossing, twisting, and circling. Fourteen tubs went every which way at the same time, providing endless thrills. Admission was fifteen cents.

Conclusion

For future generations, a time capsule was buried under the Westinghouse Building at the fair with the hope that people in the year 6939 will be able to get an idea of what life was like in 1939. The capsule was torpedo shaped and was 7 1/2 feet long and about 8 1/2 inches in diameter. Included inside were several small articles: samples of fabric, metals, and plastics; numerous books, essays, and pictures reproduced on microfilm; newsreels with instructions; and a key to the English language. There was also a lady's hat stuffed to preserve its shape.

President Roosevelt declared about the fair, "It is an inspiring thing for nations and communities to have high objectives, to unite their energies in self-appraisal, and boldly plan for the future. The New York World's Fair is a challenge to all Americans who believe in the destiny of this nation....it will be a memorable and historic Fair, one that will profoundly influence our national life for many years to come."

Fair visitors brought home many remembrances as souvenirs of their exciting visit to the New York World's Fair in 1939. The photographs in this book give you an idea of the numerous and imaginative items fair visitors could choose as their "take home" memory of a fun adventure.

Opposite page: George Washington statue and flags poster by Polygraphic Co. of America. $600.

Globe and T&P scene, by Grinnell Litho Co. $900.

93

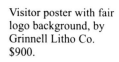

Visitor poster with fair logo background, by Grinnell Litho Co. $900.

Peace and
Freedom by
Polygraphic Co.
of America,
1940. $500.

GOODRICH WORLD'S FAIR EXHIBITS

The Goodrich Arena is bathed in floodlights

The tower that guides World's Fair visitors to the Goodrich Arena

The two front entrances to the Goodrich Arena

NEW YORK WORLD'S FAIR

Jimmie Lynch and his Great Dane drive a car from a saddle

Jimmie Lynch gets caught in a tight spot—between two hostesses

The "Guillotine", where Silvertowns prove they really can take punishment

S. B. Robertson, Goodrich President, Jimmie Lynch, D. M. Goodrich, Chairman of the Goodrich Board, and A. B. Newhall, Executive Vice President

Lynch's most daring feat — hurdling a truck at 60 miles an hour

Will your battery take care of all these needs?

Safety in the skies — Goodrich airplane de-icers keep wings clear of ice in cold weather

Goodrich Dealers meet — Sam Rush, whose service station borders the World's Fair greets George Hippard of Houston, Texas

Strength! A 4800 lb. load suspended by 4½-inches of rubber

Raw materials from throughout the world go into Goodrich products

Service plus style in Goodrich Footwear for the entire family

Thousands thrill at Jimmie Lynch's Driving Feats

Rubber "springs" for the "Car Of Tomorrow" — another Goodrich development

No wonder the crowd gasps!

A Goodrich hostess explains the Anode process of manufacturing rubber gloves

GOLDEN GATE INTERNATIONAL EXPOSITION

The Goodrich exhibit at The Golden Gate International Exposition is located in this beautiful building, "Vacationland". Here vacationists see what is new in the world of rubber

Visitors see Farm Service, airplane, Seal-o-matic and truck tire displays as well as the famous "Guillotine" test

The entrance to the Goodrich exhibit with the famous "Guillotine" in the center of the display area

Viewed from another angle, exhibit visitors see interesting pictures of some of the 39,000 rubber products made by Goodrich

96

Lehigh Valley Railroad poster announcing dance, 1939. $300.

Lehigh Valley Railroad poster announcing closing day events, 1939. $300.

The Shuler Sister's Wonder Bakery photo certificate, $250; shown with original 1939 Wonder Bread wrapper, $200.

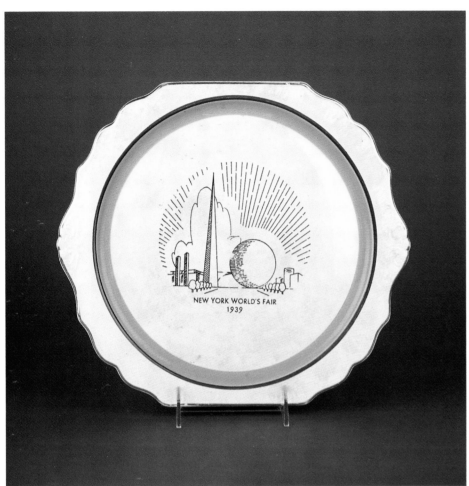

Scalloped plate by Atlas China, 1939. $125.

Pink and white plate made especially for
Tiffany & Co. for New York Fair, 1939;
pictures of modern New York. $250.

12 1/2" round platter by Edwin Knowles, 1939. $225.

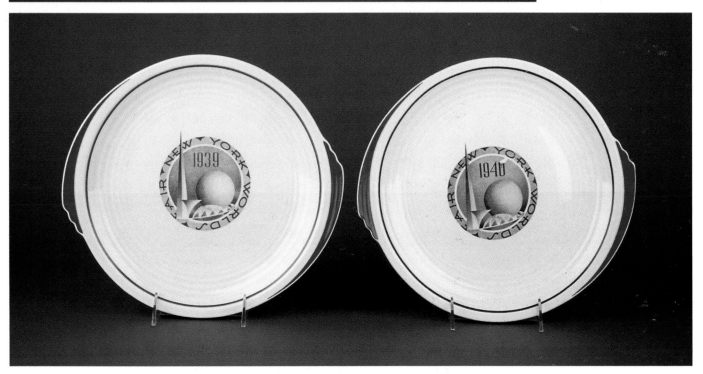

12" Art Deco plates by Edwin Knowles China Co., 1939 and 1940. $150 each.

Left to right: the George Washington Plate, blue, 1939, by Scammell's Lamberton China Co, $250; 1939 plate by Homer Laughlin China Co., $275.

J&G Meakin, England, matching blue and pink plates for 1939. $200 each.

Left to right: 1939 plate by Cronin China Co., $150; matching bowl by Paden City Pottery Co., $250.

Fiesta Ware plates depicting potters, manufactured at the American Potter Exhibit at 1939 World's Fair, $100; one still in original box, $150.

Miniatures from the American Potter Exhibit at 1939 fair; vase, $100; creamers depicting George and Martha Washington, $150; Four Seasons nut cup dishes, $200 for all.

Cobalt blue teapot by Hall China Co., 1939. $350.

Cobalt blue pretzel ashtray, for the Ballantine Inn at the World's Fair. Scammell's Lamberton China Co., 1939. $175.

1939 small, medium, and large teapots by Porcelier China Co., $250, $300, $350 respectively; shown with large water pitcher, $250.

1939 miniature tea set (teapot, creamer, sugar) and water pitcher. $500 for set.

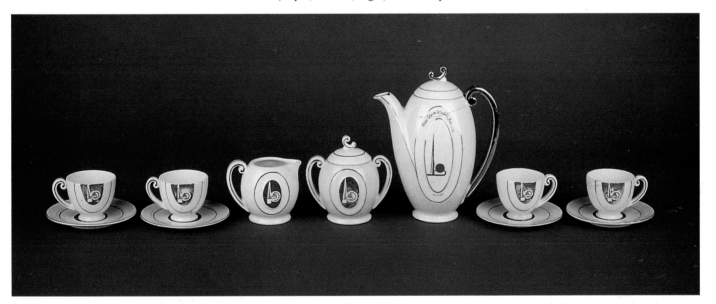

1939 Art Deco tea set, with pot, sugar, creamer, and four cups and saucers. $900.

Japan hand-painted ware: cup, saucer, candy dishes, and vases. $75 each.

Top: Heineken large pottery beer stein, 1939, $500; Heineken Delft pottery plaque, 1939, $500.

Center: Stoneware water pitcher with six matching tumblers. $900.

Left: Embossed green pottery mug, with handle, 1939. $150.

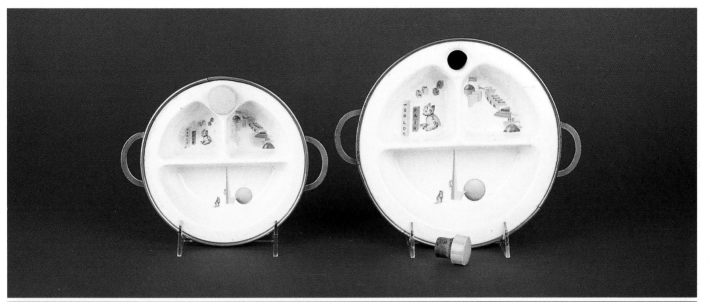

Top: Baby dishes with ceramic compartments set in stainless steel casing with compartment for warm water to keep the food warm. Large, $300; small, $200.

Center: Rectangular Lusterware tray, made in Japan, 1939, $150; Lusterware milk pitcher, made in Japan, 1939, $225.

Bottom: Lusterware covered sugar bowl, made in Japan, 1939, $150; Lusterware teapot, made in Japan, 1939, $275.

105

From left: Lusterware open vase, made in Japan, 1939, $150; Lusterware urn on pedestal with swan handles, made in Japan, 1939, $300; Lusterware vase, made in Japan, 1939, $175.

1940 carafe, gilt top, made in Japan. $300.

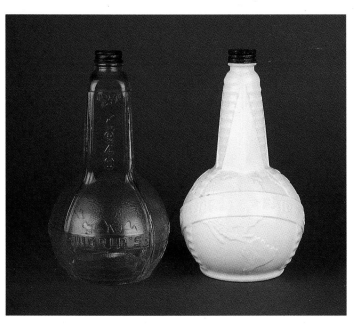

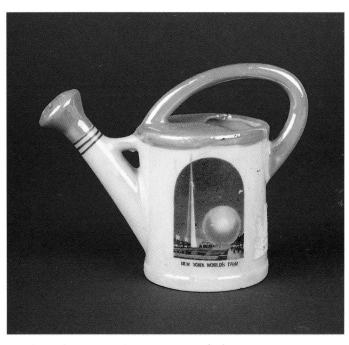

Clear glass vinegar bottle, 1939, $150; milk glass vinegar bottle, 1939, $50.

Lusterware miniature watering can, 1939, made in Japan. $75.

Large cup and saucer, New York Fair, made in Japan with hand-painted decorations. $150.

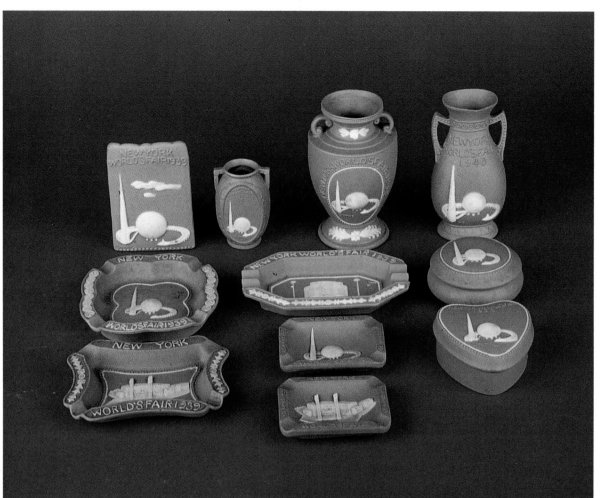

Wedgwood-type pottery in Wedgwood blue: ashtrays, vases, and jars, made in Japan for New York World's Fair, 1939. $50 each.

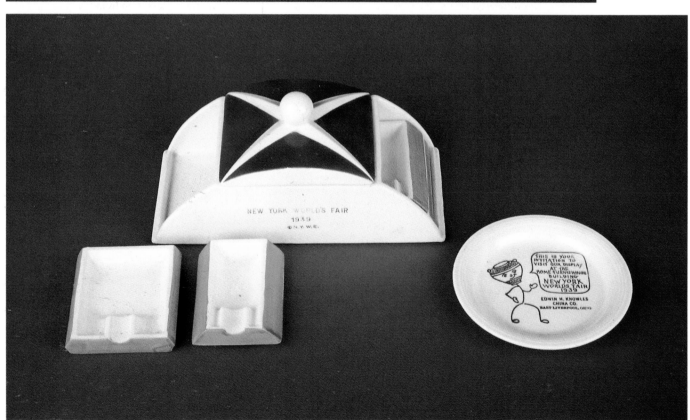

1939 ceramic cigarette holder with four ashtrays, $150; miniature ashtray advertising for Edwin Knowles China Co. at the Home Furnishings Building, 1939, $75.

From left: frosted glass dome lamp, 1939, $350; amber glass lamp with decal depicting Horticultural Exhibit, 1939, $300; blue glass lamp with decal depicting Hall of Marine Transportation, 1939, $300; wood and glass lamp from the Electric Utilities Exhibits at 1939 fair, $750.

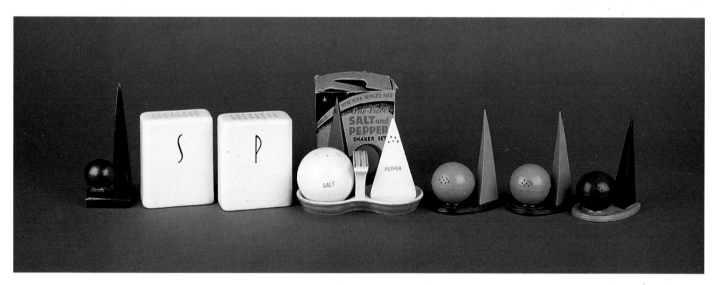

From left: T&P metal paperweight, $50; ceramic salt and pepper shaker set, $100; two-piece salt and pepper shaker set in holder, made in Japan, $100; three plastic salt and pepper shaker sets made by Emeloid Co., $50 each, one with original box, $100.

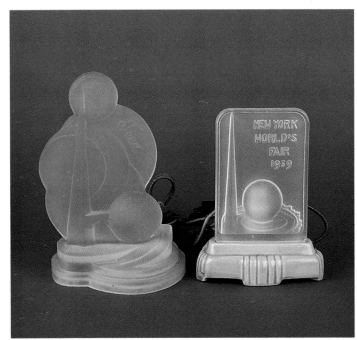

Frosted glass lamp, Lalique-type boudoir lamp, $500; ceramic and frosted glass boudoir lamp, 1939, $400.

From left: brass lantern, battery operated, 1939, $150; light bulb from General Electric Exhibit, 1939, $300; frosted, battery-operated lantern, 1939, $175.

Back row, from left: Goodrich tire ashtray, 1940, $75; two Bakelite ashtrays in black and brown, $50 each. Front row, from left: brass ashtray, 1939, $35; glass ashtray in original box, $75; glass ashtray, $35; round brass and glass ashtray, $50; Firestone tire ashtray, $75; square glass ashtray, $35.

Scalloped plate commemorating 1939 fair showing view of major New York City buildings, by Mason's China Co., England. $200.

Souvenir plate from Brazil exhibit, 1939, $100; demitasse cup and saucer from Brazil exhibit for Brazilian Coffee, $125; candy dish from Le Restaurant Francais at 1939 fair, $75.

Opposite page:
Top: Set of embossed drinking glasses from Canada Dry in original box, 1939. $300.

Center: Set of eight embossed fruit juice glasses in original holder, made by Libby Glass Co. $250.

Bottom: Three large water glasses depicting Cosmetic Building, Communications Building, and Marine Transportation Building, $50 each; two juice glasses, $50 each.

Set of twelve embossed glass coasters in original box, 1939, made in Holland, $150; replica of the original 200" disc from the Glass Center, Corning, New York, $100.

Ovington Department Store catalogue, $50; large green Lenox vase, $600; green Lenox salt and pepper shakers, $250; green Lenox cigarette holder, $300; cobalt blue flared Lenox vase, $600; yellow Lenox cone vase, $400; Lenox white cigarette holder, $300; yellow and white Lenox cigarette boxes, $350 each.

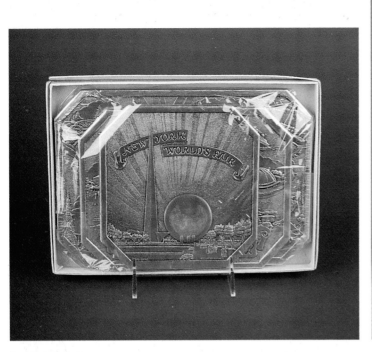 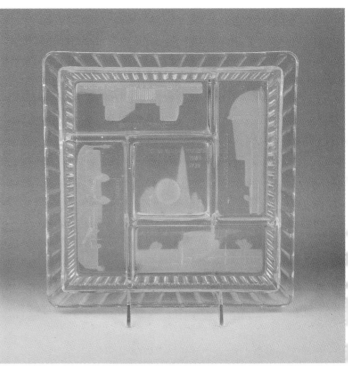

Opposite page:

Top left: Set of three 1939 hotplates in original box. $100.

Top right: Clear and frosted glass relish dish, 1939. $150.

Bottom: Glass ice bucket, 1939, $150; glass water pitcher depicting 1939 Theme Building, $175.

Above: Back row: powder jars with music box. Second from left, 1940; all others, 1939. $175 each. Front row: glass powder jar with hand-painted top, 1939, $150; metal powder jar with 1939 fair logo, $75; same in green, $75; glass powder jar with 1939 fair logo, $100.

Right: Large T&P bank with thermometer. $250.

Below: Back row, from left: large T&P bank with thermometer, $250; wooden barrel bank, 1939, $75; Esso Gasoline glass globe bank, 1939, $200; Esso Gasoline large glass block bank with original wrapper, 1939, $250; small glass block bank, made at the Glass Center, 1939 fair, $150; large tin T&P bank with thermometer, 1939, $250. Front row, from left: miniature metal luggage bank depicting Federal Building, 1939, $225; Remington typewriter bank from the Remington Rand Hall, 1939, $100; stainless steel bank with Federal Building logo, 1939, $225.

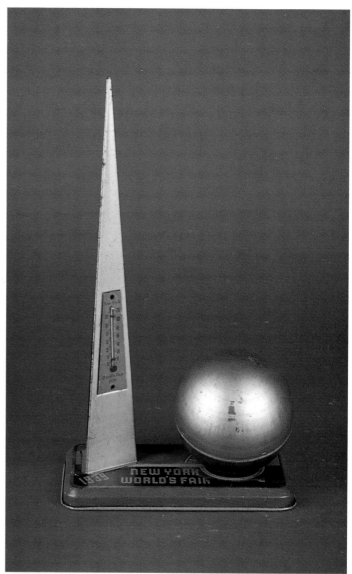

Set of New York World's Fair (1939-40) silverware by William Rogers Co., including knives, forks, spoons, serving pieces, and butter knives in wooden box. $1,000.

Set of twelve teaspoons by Rogers Manufacturing Co. in original wooden box, 1939, $250; set of twelve teaspoons in original mailing boxes by Rogers Manufacturing Co., $250.

Tin tray depicting 1939 World's Fair buildings. $200.

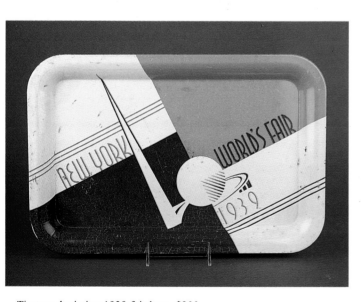

Tin tray depicting 1939 fair logo. $200.

Tin advertising tray for D'Oro Coffee, 1939. $150.

1939 Metal serving tray, $175; shown with seven coasters depicting, left to right: Aviation Building, Federal Building, Maritime Building, T&P, Ford Building, United States Steel, and Music Hall, $25 each.

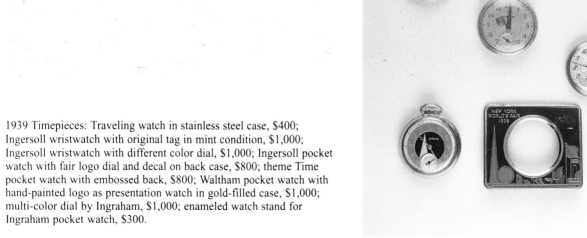

1939 Timepieces: Traveling watch in stainless steel case, $400; Ingersoll wristwatch with original tag in mint condition, $1,000; Ingersoll wristwatch with different color dial, $1,000; Ingersoll pocket watch with fair logo dial and decal on back case, $800; theme Time pocket watch with embossed back, $800; Waltham pocket watch with hand-painted logo as presentation watch in gold-filled case, $1,000; multi-color dial by Ingraham, $1,000; enameled watch stand for Ingraham pocket watch, $300.

118

Desk clock with World's Fair logo, 1939, $350; wooden electric clock by Waltham, $600; electric clock with 1939 World's Fair logo dial, $500.

From left: metal desk clock with 1939 World's Fair logo, $300; wooden desk clock with 1939 fair logo, $250; brass desk clock with 1939 fair logo, $275.

Stereovues with view glasses in original mailer, $100; Third Dimension photograph album, with viewer and "stereocards" in original box, 1939. $300.

Leather desk pad, $300; oversize pencil with eraser, $100; flashlight pencil, $100; collapsible pencil, $50; two-tone fountain pen, $100; orange and blue pen/pencil combination, $100; red fountain pen, $75; white pen/pencil combination with fair logo on barrel, $100; oversize dip pen in original box, $150.

One hundred movie views with camera and film in original box, 1939. $150.

Simple brass desk calendar, 1939. $100.

From left: 1939 Anchor inkwell depicting Administration Building with original glass insert, $250; glass inkwell depicting Administration Building, $100; 1939 T&P metal inkwell, $150.

From left: two Univex World's Fair model cameras, 1939, with box, $300 each; Bullet Camera in plastic by Eastman Kodak Co., 1939, $400; box camera in plastic with 1939 fair logo by Eastman Kodak Co., $400.

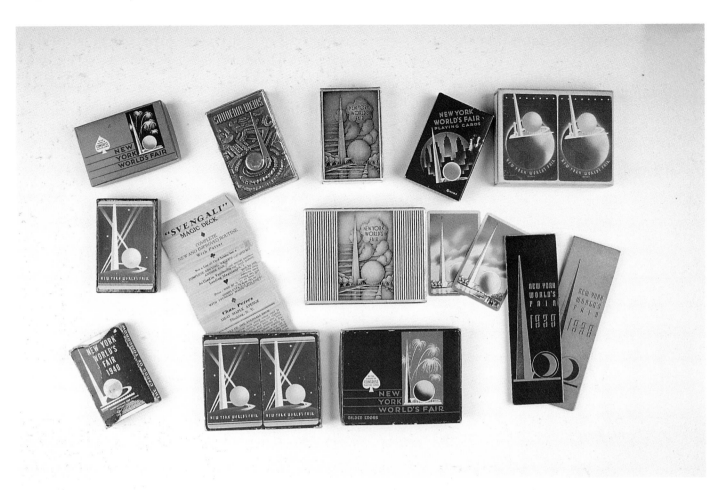

World's Fair playing cards, 1939: logo deck, $100; World of Tomorrow deck, $100; logo deck in purple, pink, and yellow, $100; logo deck with city skyline, $100; double deck with fair logo, $175; deck with fair logo in burgundy, $100; double deck with fair logo, $175; bridge tally pads, $50 each; magic deck with instructions, $150; double deck with fair logo, $175; double deck with gilded edges by Congress Playing Card Co. $175.

Snow dome paperweight, 1939, $175; brass-plated T&P paperweight, 1939, $75.

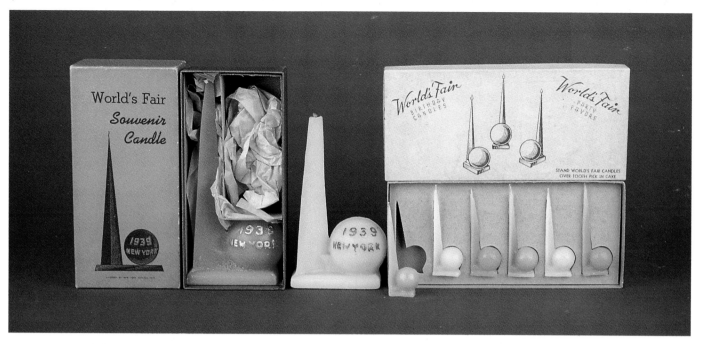

T&P souvenir candle in original box, $175; T&P white candle, $75; six birthday candles in original box, $175.

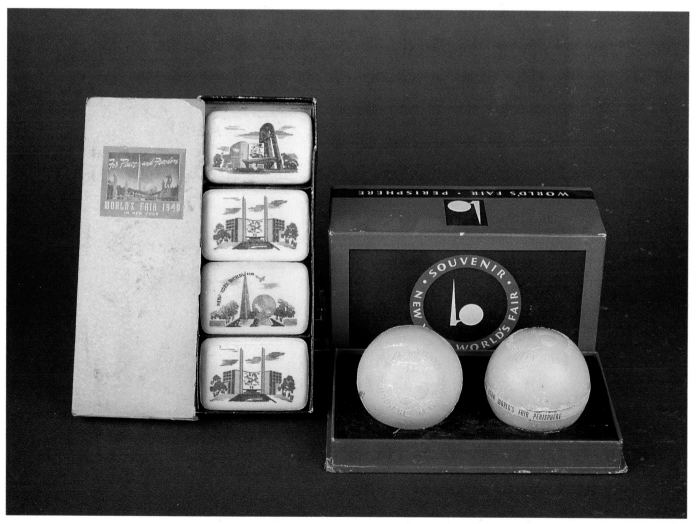

Four bars of soap in original box, 1940, $200; two soap balls in original box, $200.

Above: Ladies celluloid hand mirror with scenes of 1939 fair buildings, $150; men's electric shaver from the 1939 Remington Rand Hall, $200.

Below: Two souvenir Bakelite T&P thermometer sets in original mailing boxes, and one pencil sharpener. $125 each.

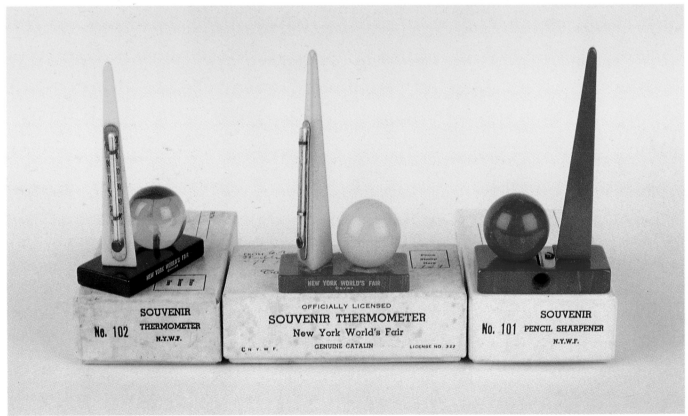

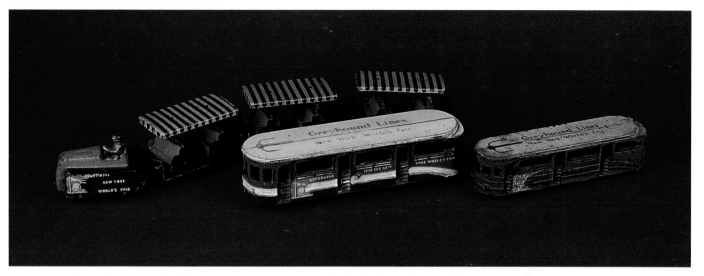

Four-piece tram with driver, made by Arcade Toy Co., $750; Greyhound bus made by Arcade Toy Co., 1939, small size $400, medium size, $600.

Plastic T&P puzzle in original box, $100; plywood jigsaw picture puzzle, $100; Trupe Girl Scout card game, $125; New York World's Fair-ly-gig magic piece, $100; and Patriotic Pyramid Puzzle, $150.

RCA table model radio with original tubes, 1939. $2,000.

Opposite page:
Remington Rand portable typewriter, made especially for the 1939
World's Fair, in original carrying case. $1,000.

From left: Dandy Goodwill doll, $400; wooden clown doll, $800; Phillip Morris doll, 1939, $300.

Macy's Toyland Dutch girl doll in original box, made by Alexander Doll Co., 1939. $500.

Top: Peter Coddle at the New York World's Fair, a game by Parker Bros., $200. Bottom: wooden puzzle set in original box by Puzzle Craft, $150.

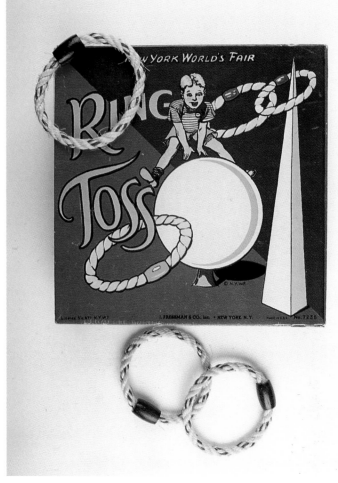

Ring Toss game with wooden T&P stand and rope rings, mint, in original box, 1939. $800.

Bobby and Betty's Trip to the New York World's Fair, 1939, a game by Parker Brothers. $600.

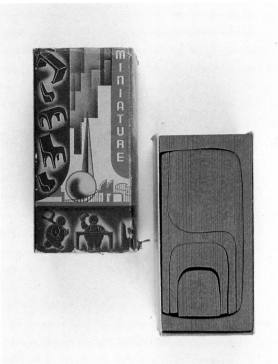

Uncle Foster's World's Fair Game, 1939, in different color boxes. $150 each.

Set of miniature furniture in original box, 1939. $200.

Bingo game set, in original box, 1939, by Whitman Publishing Co. $200.

Wooden perfume box from Coty, 1940, $50; T&P perfume holder from Rubicon, $50; same in original box, $75; covered wagon for Caravan Perfume, 1939, $125; perfume holder with three bottles of Cardinal Perfume, $150; and three Rubicon perfume bottles in original box, $300.

Rubicon Perfume T&P in original box, $150; three miniature perfume bottles, $25 each; Cardinal Perfume holder in shape of books, $75; round glass perfume holder by Duvink with three bottles, $100; Merrie England perfume bottles, $35 each.

From left: Dunhill cigarette lighter in original box with T&P, $500; brass cigarette pack holder, $75; plastic cigarette pack holder, $50; pair of Bakelite cigarette boxes showing Toffenetti Candy Co., $75 each; two hand-carved wooden pipes inscribed "World's Fair 1939," $150 each; tabletop cigarette lighter, $75.

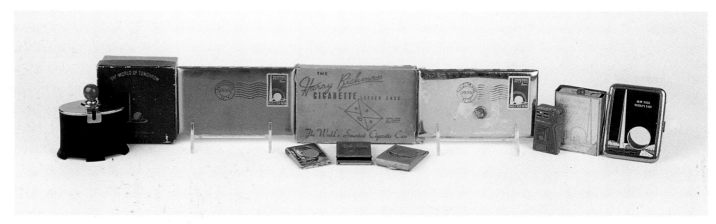

Desktop lighter by Coe & Gregg in original box, $150; cigarette letter case by Harry Richman in silver and goldplate, $150; matches showing Theme Center, $20; brass matchpack holder, $35; match pack holder in hammered brass, $40; pocket lighter, $50; cigarette pack holder, $50; and enameled brass cigarette case, $100.

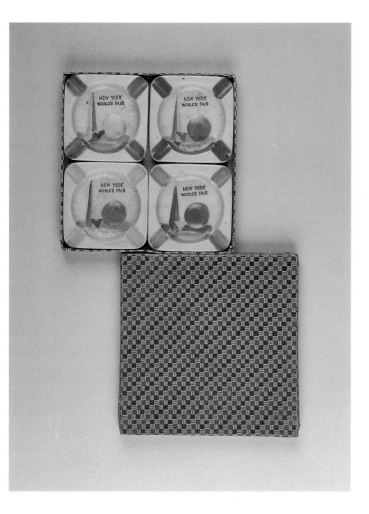

Set of miniature ceramic ashtrays, made in Japan, 1939. $100.

Blue metal cigarette case with fair logo, $75; fair cigarette case with enamel inlay of fair logo, 1939, $125.

Opposite page and this page: Assorted ladies compacts by manufacturers including Zell, Elgin-American, Girey, and others, 1939-40. $50-$300 each.

Sterling silver Incubator Baby presentation cup for Shirley Ann at 1939 fair, $300; small silverplate baby cup, 1939, $150.

Futurama booklet from 1939, with button. $25 each piece.

Fiberglass Wonder Book made at the Glass Center, 1939, complete with booklets and pure glass items made at the Glass Center. $250.

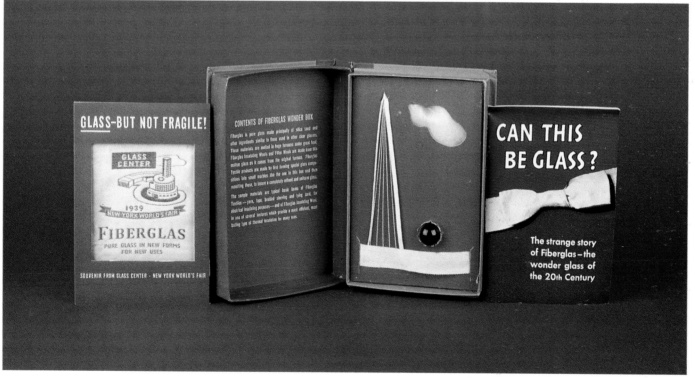

From left: large reverse painting on glass picture frame with T&P logo, $250; same in smaller size, $200; small silverplated picture frame with T&P logo, $200.

Clip-top brocade T&P and floral design purse, 1939, $250; 1939 handmade beaded bag, $350.

Opposite page: Rayon pillow sham, 1939, $75; silk handkerchief holder, $50; reverse painted purse mirror, $50.

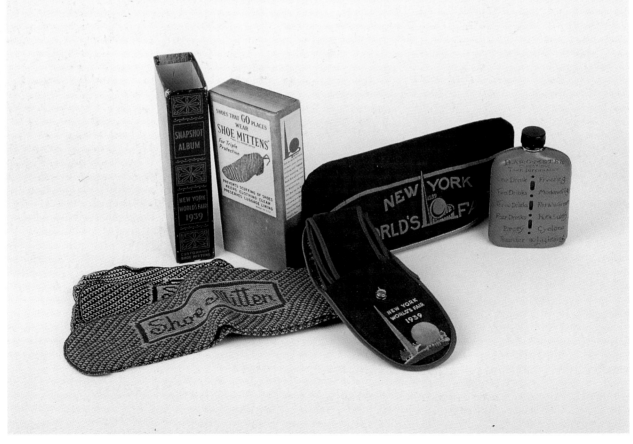

Large cookie tin with embossed logo, 1939. $100.

Opposite page:
Top: Leather holder for stockings and handkerchief, 1939. $100.

Bottom: Shoe mittens in original cardboard box, 1939, $100; felt cap
with 1939 fair logo, $50; leather-covered flask, $75; felt traveling
slippers in original case, $100.

Opposite page:
Leather bookcover, 1939, $75; leather-handled clothes brush with embossed logo, $125.

Packet of souvenir postcards from the USSR Pavilion, $100; shown with large book of Soviet paintings from USSR Pavilion, 1939, $500.

Top row, from left: leatherette telephone directory, 1939, $100; leather autograph book, 1940, $125; leather diary, $150. Bottom row, from left: green leather covered writing pad, $75; pocket leather writing pad advertising Calvert Whiskey, $75; New Testament souvenir edition by New York Bible Society, $100; brown leather covered writing pad, $75.

144

Opposite page:
Sheet music for 1940 music, "When the Spirit Moves Me." $40.

World's Fair sheet music from 1939, "For Peace and Freedom" and "The Gates of Old New York Swing Open to the Fair." $50 each.

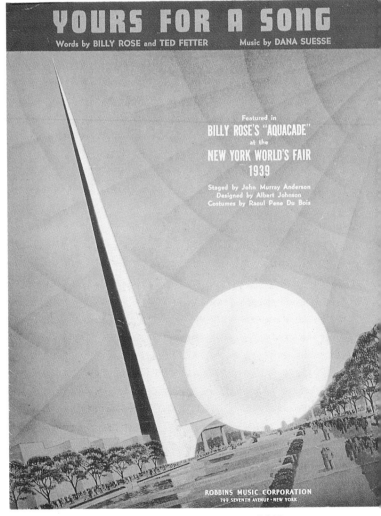

Sheet music for 1939 music, "Yours for a Song." $40.

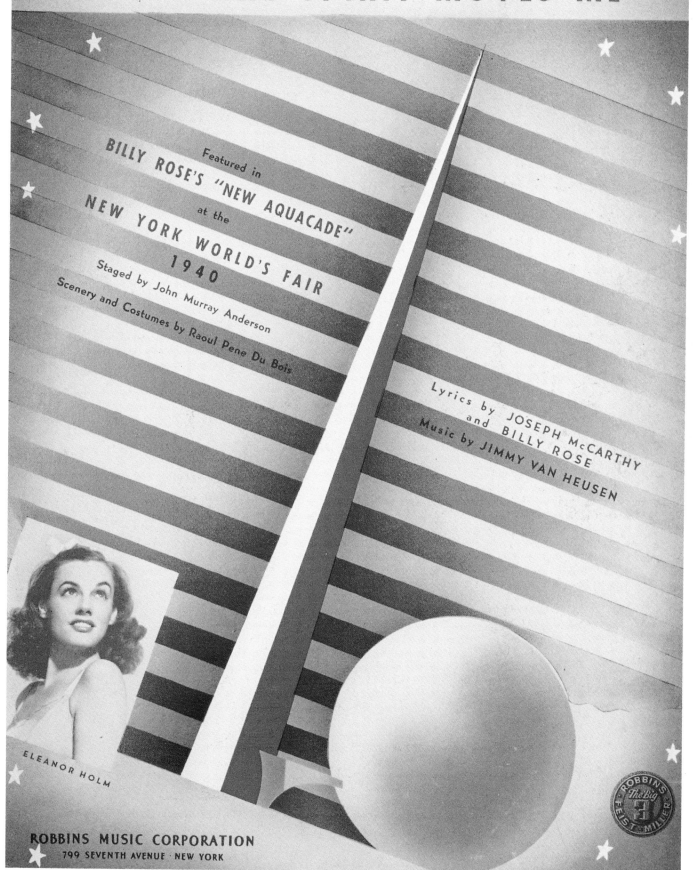

Original photo, "Contrasts," 1939, by S.B. Johnson. $200.

Original photo, "Design," 1939, by S.B. Johnson. $200.

Original photo, "New York World's Fair," 1939, by S.B. Johnson. $200.

Original photo showing theme center, 1939, by S.B. Johnson. $200.

Opposite page:
From top: children's cut-and-paste book, complete in mint condition, $300; France souvenir book, limited edition, $250; Stoeger Catalogue, $150.

The Time Capsule, Limited Edition #114, $500; Official Guidebook,
1939, hardbound, $75; World's Fair Building Code book, $100;
Miracle of Glass, $50.

Toy Catalogue from the Gilbert Co. with original mailing envelope,
1939, $150; commemorative coins in original holder, $150.

From bottom right: large bronze medal with T&P and George Washington, $150; enameled pocket mirror, $100; police badge, $300; enameled fire department badge, $500; matching lieutenant hat pin, $300.

Sewing items: boxed sewing kit from J&P Coats Co., $100; leather pouch with assorted needles, $50; orange and blue ribbon from the Wanamaker Store, $100; paper sewing kit with assorted needles, $50; World's Fairest coat buttons, $50; boxed sewing kit, $75.

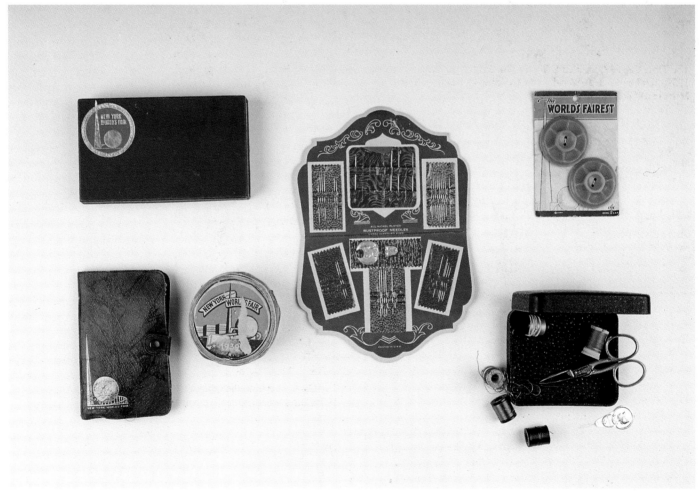

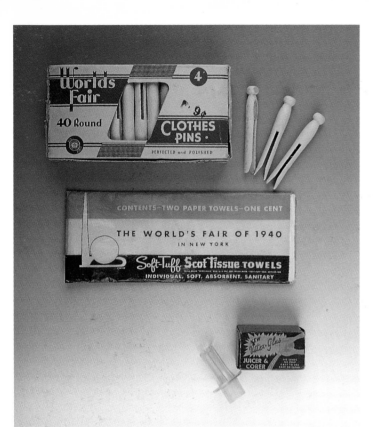

Opposite page:
Celluloid, metal, and wooden pin-back buttons, 1939. $25-100 each.

Forty fair clothespins in original box, $150; two paper towels by Scot Tissue in original envelope, $50; Vitex-glas Juicer and Corer in original box, 1939, $50.

Assorted ladies jewelry including bracelets, pins, and lockets. $50-200 each.

Celluloid pin-back buttons and ladies jewelry, 1939. $25-100 each.

Celluloid and metal pin-back buttons, 1939. $40-150 each.

Opposite page:
Bakelite pin backs, $50 each; metal bookmarks, $40 each; Bakelite and metal lighters, $100 each; employee badge, $100; black Bakelite bookmarks, $40 each; set of uniform buttons, $40 each; square employee badge, 1940, $75; horseshoe badge, $50; Russian Pavilion pins, $100; assorted jewelry, $50 each; pocket knives, $75 each.

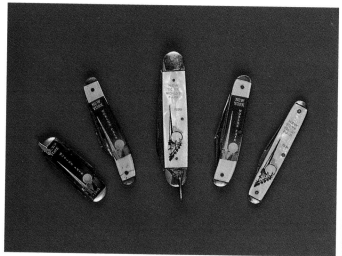

Pocket knives from 1939. $50-150 each.

1939 card table in mint condition. $500.

BIBLIOGRAPHY

Books

Bishop, Glenn A. and Paul T. Gilbert. *Chicago's Progress, A Review of the World's Fair City.* Chicago: Bishop Publishing Company, 1933.

Hill, Henry Chase and Will H. Johnston. *The New Wonder Book of Knowledge, New York World's Fair Edition.* New York: The John C. Winston Company, 1940.

Official Guide, Book of the Fair. Chicago: The Cuneo Press, Inc., 1933.

Official Guide Book, New York World's Fair. New York: Expositions Publications, Inc., 1939.

Periodicals

Official World's Fair Weekly, Opening Week, A Century of Progress International Exposition. Chicago: The Cuneo Press, Inc., 1933.

Opposite page:
Top: Five woven silk souvenir pictures showing scenes from fair, made in Switzerland, 1939. $50 each.

Bottom: Felt pennants, 1939: green and yellow, $100; black and orange, $75; yellow and purple, $100.

INDEX